ALL RISE
THE AARON JUDGE STORY
BILL GUTMAN

Post Hill
PRESS

A POST HILL PRESS BOOK
ISBN: 978-1-68261-704-5
ISBN (eBook): 978-1-68261-705-2

All Rise—The Aaron Judge Story

Post Hill Press
New York • Nashville
posthillpress.com

Published in the United States of America

CONTENTS

CONTENTS

INTRODUCTION

"ALL RISE!" THAT WAS A call heard all over baseball during the 2017 season because of one man. Aaron Judge, the strapping, six-foot-seven, 282-pound rookie outfielder with the New York Yankees captured the imagination of fans everywhere by hitting the highest, longest, *loudest* home runs seen in years. And that wasn't the only reason this 25-year-old rookie quickly became the face of baseball in the first half of the season, bursting onto the scene like perhaps no other young player before him.

The excitement generated by Aaron Judge wasn't only because he could hit the ball higher and farther than anyone else in the game, but also the fact that he was all athlete. One of the biggest men ever to play Major League Baseball, he was also an outstanding right fielder, had a great throwing arm, and could run—even to the point of stealing a base. On top of that, he had a quick smile and was totally humble and friendly, always ready to sign autographs for the fans and engage with the media. Yet he would politely refuse to brag about himself or his accomplishments, deflecting many questions to the team, his team-mates, and his desire to win.

On top of that, he never showed anyone up on the field. He could hit a 450-foot home run and he would just put his head down and run. There were no fancy bat flips, no posing at home plate to admire his hand-iwork, no glaring at the opposing pitchers. He would just circle the bases and return to the dugout. All unique in the look-at-me sporting world of today.

It was, however, Aaron's tremendous production over the first half of the season that generated an enormous amount of buzz throughout the game. With teammates Gary Sanchez and Didi Gregorius missing most of the first month of the season with injuries, it was Aaron who pretty much carried the Yankees offense. He was not only leading the league in home runs, but hitting over .300 and driving in runs in bunches. Fans all over the league began coming out to ballparks early just to watch him take batting practice because of the mammoth shots he would hit. And soon the Yankees set up a special section of seats in right field at Yankee Stadium called "The Judge's Chambers." A select number of fans sat there each game, donning judge robes, some wearing long white powdered wigs, and carrying signs that read **ALL RISE**. All rise when a real judge enters a courtroom, and it seems that all fans rise to their feet when Judge steps to the plate.

By the time the All-Star break rolled around, Aaron had hit 30 home runs, was batting .329, and had driven home 66 runs—tremendous production for a first-year player. He was the American League's starting right fielder in the All-Star Game and also entered in the Home Run Derby, held the night before the game. He put on an incredible show, winning the competition by slamming 47 home runs, almost effortlessly. By that time, everyone wanted to see him, hoping he would hit one of his patented, long home runs. He had become so popular and intriguing that he was already considered the face of baseball, a designation rookies rarely receive.

Then a sudden and deep batting slump during the first six weeks following the All-Star break really tested Aaron's mettle. He might have bent, but he didn't break, never making excuses and still going out every day with a positive attitude. Perhaps part of it was fatigue from the long season and all the hoopla surrounding him. Or it could have been a sore shoulder, which he was icing after every game. But his approach to his game never changed. He always smiled and said he was ready to play. With the Yankees fighting for a division title, Aaron had a rebirth in September, his final month of the season mirroring his first half. Once again he was one of baseball's top sluggers and run producers.

Just who is this gentle giant who caught the fancy of the baseball world? Would you believe he's a kid hailing from a tiny California town known primarily for its yearly crop of cherries and its friendly people? What were the odds that this kid would grow up and make it all the way to Yankee Stadium, let alone electrify Major League Baseball with his talent, personality, and passion for the game? This is how it all happened. This is *The Aaron Judge Story*.

CHAPTER ONE

THE EARLY YEARS

♛

LINDEN, CALIFORNIA, IN THE CENTRAL part of the state, is a small town with a population that today might be hovering around 2,000 people. The 2010 census listed the number at 1,794, definitely making Linden a tiny speck on a very large map. What had always distinguished Linden over the years was the annual Cherry Festival, held every summer. Being known mainly for its cherry crop was another thing that earmarked Linden as Small Town, USA. Only, these days, something else has been added, something that has put Linden on the national map. For this small California town is also the home of the

New York Yankees sensational young slugger, Aaron Judge.

It's a long way from Linden to Yankee Stadium in the Bronx, where Aaron Judge began electrifying crowds—and the entire Major League Baseball world—in 2017. But young Aaron made the journey from Linden to New York almost seamlessly—overcoming a number of bumps in the road—and he's quick to credit his family as well as his upbringing in Linden, a place he'll always call home.

Though Linden is just 45 miles from the state capital of Sacramento, it has always retained a small-town atmosphere. It was settled originally by Italian immigrants who became known as truck farmers because, in the 1920s and 1930s, they would grow produce and then truck their goods to San Francisco to sell them. In the ensuing years, however, the town became known for the bumper crops of cherries it produced annually.

On a personal level, the people of Linden were close and friendly, and always looked after each other. "I think everybody's out here for the same reason," said Eric Schmidt, a longtime neighbor of the Judge family. "We want to raise kids, to have a chance at that American dream or whatever you want to call it. It's kind of like Mayberry in that way."

Mayberry was the idyllic fictional town from the 1950s' *The Andy Griffith Show*, a popular sitcom of the time. It remains to this day a symbol of small-town Americana, where caring people often help each other and children grow up without the many potential dangers of today's world. It may be hard for some to believe, but the people of Linden, for the most part, live that way today. And that's how Aaron Judge grew up.

Aaron was born in Linden on April 26, 1992, but there was an immediate twist to the story, one that would help shape Aaron into the man he would become. When he was just one day old, he was adopted by Patty and Wayne Judge, both Linden residents and teachers. They had already adopted one son, John, and now Aaron would make their family complete.

For Patty Judge, having her two sons has always been a blessing. "We're very proud of both our boys. Aaron's older brother, John, is teaching English in Korea. I always said it was all meant to be." Wayne Judge has said that there was a miracle when they adopted Aaron.

"I've always felt that they kind of picked me," was the way Aaron put it. "I feel that God was the one that matched us together."

Young Aaron grew up in a home that emphasized education and respect. He has said of his parents, "They taught me right from wrong, how to treat people, treat them with respect. They also encouraged me to always go the extra mile and put in extra work. They really molded me into the person I am today." And as far as education was concerned, his schoolwork always came first, and, from an early age, he knew what that would eventually mean.

"Because my parents were teachers, they were always big into going to college. That would make a later decision very easy for me."

There was yet another issue that Wayne and Patty Judge knew would have to be addressed at some point. It was resolved when Aaron was about ten or eleven years old. He recalled just how it happened.

"I realized [my parents and I] didn't look alike, and one day I just said, 'I don't look like you, Mom. I don't look like you, Dad. What's going on?' They then came out and told me I was adopted. They answered all my questions, and I said, 'Okay, that's fine with me.

You're still my mom, the only mom I know. You're still my dad, the only dad I know.'"

Learning they were adopted can be a daunting discovery for youngsters. Some, as they grow older, begin looking for their biological parents and always want more answers. But Aaron was smart enough to realize he was in a great situation, the best one for him, and that was good enough.

"Some kids grow in their mom's stomach," he said, making it simple to understand. "I grew in my mom's heart. She always showed me love and compassion ever since I was a little baby. I never needed to think differently or wonder about anything."

To that end, Aaron has never had any contact with his biological parents. And while it is apparent he is biracial, he has also never spoken of his ethnicity in public. He loved his life with his parents and loved growing up in Linden. As a child, he couldn't ask for anything more. But soon, something else would become a big part of Aaron Judge's life: sports.

Like so many kids Aaron loved to play ball. It didn't matter then whether it was baseball, football, or basketball. He played all of them often with his friends, and it didn't take very long for his parents to see that sports was something special to him.

"His mother and I just wanted him to be a really good person," Wayne Judge said. "But we knew, from [when he was at] a very young age, as soon as we put a ball in his hand, that he had a lot of natural talent."

It happens that way with the most talented kids. You can see it immediately. Some parents tend to become overexcited about a child's early ability and begin to envision college scholarships and maybe even a professional career in the future. Today that can mean millions of dollars for those who make it to the pro ranks, and parents begin to push them, picking out their son's best sport right away and urging him to play only that one to the exclusion of the others. It's a bad situation in that many kids burn out early and quit. Some begin to get what they call repetitive motion injuries from playing just the one sport all year round. But Patty and Wayne Judge never did that. They wanted Aaron to have fun and enjoy playing all the sports with his friends. But there was always another hard and fast rule he had to follow.

If he didn't maintain a certain GPA in his studies he would lose the "privilege" of playing both sports and the video games that kids love. True to form, he never lost that privilege because his GPA was always right where it was supposed to be. In other words, he always had his priorities straight and never wavered.

The early years in Linden made an impression on Aaron and he quickly realized how lucky he was to be there. "It was just a close-knit community," he said. "Everywhere you went you'd see someone you knew on the street corner. That was the cool thing about growing up there. I knew everybody, and everybody was my friend. Everyone was looking out for each other, and, as far as I'm concerned, there was no better place to grow up."

Aaron was also growing in another way during his teenage years. He was getting taller and taller, by far the tallest kid on his Little League team and, soon after, shooting past the six-foot mark. But he still didn't stop there. He continued to grow, and it was soon apparent he was going to be exceptionally tall. In fact, he was well over six feet tall when he entered Linden High School in the fall of 2006. And by the time he graduated, he was already at his full height of six-foot-seven.

Eric Schmidt, who was the Judge family's next-door neighbor when Aaron was growing up, remembers being surprised at how the kid next door just continued to grow.

"I'm a tall guy," Schmidt said, "so I always noticed that Aaron was getting taller and taller. Then he was taller than me and still growing. And then his body also began filling out, getting thicker and one day I just said, 'Boy, that's a good-size guy.'"

By that time, the boy who was also beginning to look like a man was totally into sports, all three of them—baseball, football, and basketball—that he would play at Linden High for three years. In the beginning, he liked all equally but thought he had a distinct advantage in one.

"Growing up, I always thought I'd be a basketball player because I was so tall," he said.

That didn't mean he had set his sights on the NBA, but he probably thought at some point that basketball could be his ticket to college. It was soon apparent, however, that he could be good enough to excel at all three. As a sophomore, he made the varsity baseball squad and after the season was named the All-Mother Lode League team's first baseman. By his junior year, he was attracting attention in all three sports and many were wondering again which one he would choose to play in college because it was becoming obvious he would be watched by recruiters in all three.

And while this was happening, Aaron was keeping his grades up and still enjoying life as a teenager with many friends in Linden. They would often hang out at Jim's Lunch, a small eatery on the corner of Main Street and High Street that was known for its one-of-a-kind hamburgers, which were always Aaron's favorite. But he also did volunteer work at St. Andrew's Church Acolyte and often performed community service with his basketball teammates. Believe it or not, the boys went around town picking up garbage.

"That was one of my favorite things to do," Aaron said. "We all got up real early, had breakfast, and then walked around the community gathering up all the garbage we could find. We had a lot of fun doing it, and it was a good bonding experience for the team."

It's not surprising that Aaron did things like picking up garbage and volunteering at church willingly. Once again, he learned those qualities from his parents. Both Wayne and Patty Judge were said to be among the most active members of their community. Aaron's mother was always one of the first to welcome people who moved to Linden and help them get acclimated to their new homes and lifestyles.

As for Aaron, his junior year at Linden High saw him as a pass-receiving tight end on the football team, a center on the basketball team, and in the spring a first baseman/pitcher with the baseball squad. Already at his full height, he weighed in at about 235 pounds then. It was pretty apparent he would fill out and become even stronger, especially if he began training as a college athlete. And by that time, the football recruiters had begun to discover him.

"In my junior year, I began getting a lot of letters from schools that wanted me for football," he said.

Among the colleges that began recruiting him were Notre Dame, Stanford, and UCLA, all big-time Division-I schools. They saw him as a strong tight end—a player athletic and fast enough to be a force as a pass receiver as well as a blocker. But something else was happening within him that not everybody knew. He was beginning to realize which sport really got his juices flowing, and it wasn't football.

"I was going to a lot of baseball camps by this time, especially in the summer, and it wasn't long before I knew this was the sport I wanted to pursue."

Many young athletes, having come to a decision like that by their junior year of high school would simply concentrate on the sport they had chosen and not play all three. But Aaron felt an obligation to the school, his town, and his teammates. Not surprisingly, he continued to be Linden High's biggest three-sport star as a senior.

In the fall of 2009, Aaron took to the gridiron for the Linden High Lions and produced an outstanding season as a tight end. He caught 54 passes for a single season school record of 959 yards and his 17 touchdown catches were also a new mark. That gave him a school record of 21 career TDs. He obviously had great size, but also good speed and a great pair of hands. He was an all-league and all-area first-team selection after the season.

Many of the fans and friends of Aaron were marveling at how good he had become. Race Geesink, who was several years younger than Aaron, had been watching him play for years.

"We were all surprised, but, at the same time, not so surprised," Geesink said, referring to Aaron's great play. "I remember saying just throw him the ball because of how big he was."

When it was time for basketball, it was more of the same. Obviously playing at the center position, Aaron again used his height, strength, and surprising agility to average 18.2 points and 12.8 rebounds a game, once more becoming a first-team All-Mother Lode League selection. He was also named to the Cal-Hi Sports Division-IV all-state team. The question rose again: Was there a basketball scholarship and pro career in his future? He certainly seemed to have a possible future in both football and basketball, especially after his fine senior season in both. But now it was time for baseball.

It didn't take long for Aaron to show that he could be totally dominant on the baseball field. Dividing his time between playing first base and pitching, he put together a brilliant season. For openers, he won the Mother Lode League Triple Crown with a .500 batting average, seven home runs, and 32 runs batted in. That wasn't all. As a pitcher, he went 9–3 for the season with a microscopic 0.88 earned run average, all while striking out 65 hitters and walking just 20. To top it off, he won the last five games he pitched.

More honors followed. Not only did the Lions win the league championship, but they made it all the way to the Sac-Joaquin Section Division-V semifinals. And Aaron once again made the all-league team. That

June he graduated from Linden High with a 3.2 GPA and, along with all his sports prowess and volunteer work, also spent two years on the student council. There was little doubt that Wayne and Patty Judge, along with the small-town atmosphere in Linden, had produced a fine young man. Then came the question of what next?

PRO BASEBALL OR COLLEGE

It was pretty much a foregone conclusion that Aaron would continue on to college. After all, his parents had put an emphasis on education all his life, and he had always done well in his studies. If he were interested in continuing to play football and perhaps even basketball, he'd obviously have a scholarship waiting. The colleges are like a minor league for young football and basketball players, giving them a chance to grow and develop as the professional teams continue to scout them. That was certainly an option. And it was also possible that he'd do the same with baseball, so he really had a big decision to make. Then, all of a sudden, something unexpected came into play.

Aaron and his parents received a phone call informing him that the Oakland A's had picked Aaron in the 30th round of the 2010 first-year player draft. That meant he could sign a professional baseball contract immediately if he chose. Major League teams often use a low draft choice to pick good high school players who may or may not make it. They don't give them much of a signing bonus and let them start by playing in rookie leagues and the low minors. A 17- or 18-year-old signing out of high school might spend years toiling in the minor leagues for little pay. Many of them never make it to the majors and then find themselves having to start over again in perhaps their mid-20s.

That was one way to look at it. If a youngster has only a baseball career on his mind he might jump at the chance, hoping to eventually make it to the majors and live out his dream while also making a lot of money. But none of that really factored into Aaron Judge's decision. In fact, for him it was the proverbial no-brainer.

"Both my parents were teachers," he said, "so they were big into kids going to college. It made my decision pretty easy. In fact, I felt like I needed to go to college. I just didn't think I was mature enough to face the real world yet."

It was a wise decision and one that was well thought-out. Aaron wasn't the type of kid who would just jump into something for which he wasn't ready. It would have been easy to fall for the flattery of being picked by a major-league team. But with his parents' guidance, he came to the quick conclusion that college was the better choice. By then he knew that baseball was the sport he wanted to pursue, so the football offers from some major schools were not really considered. When all was said and done, he decided to stay close to home and accept a baseball scholarship to California State University, Fresno, more commonly called Fresno State.

"[Aaron] is just a hometown kid," said his coach at Linden, Roy Hallenback. "He could have gone and played anywhere."

The school he chose was located in Fresno, California, not that far from Linden, so the situation was perfect for Aaron. His family and friends could easily come see him play. And, not surprisingly, Fresno coach Mike Batesole was glad to have Aaron on his Division-I baseball team. Fresno State had always had fine players, with a good number of them making it to the major leagues. Coach Batesole was taken by Aaron's size, but size alone doesn't make a baseball player. Then he started to see other things as well that made him think he had a diamond in the rough.

Every year around Thanksgiving, and long before the baseball season would begin, the coach would organize a five-on-five touch football league for his players. He felt it was a good break from their off-season conditioning program. And that's when the coach really saw how athletic Aaron Judge was.

"These guys are all Division I athletes and they couldn't touch him. When I saw him out there the first time it was like Barry Sanders quickness and agility. (Sanders was one of the all-time great NFL running backs.) And I'm going, 'This guy is really different.'"

It didn't take Coach Batesole long to realize he had a special player on his hands. He knew that Aaron had pitched in high school and obviously respected the big guy's mound ability.

"It's lucky I'm the hitting coach as well as the head coach," he said, jokingly. "If I was the pitching coach and head coach, I'd probably start getting him ready to pitch in the big leagues right now."

That wasn't all Batesole saw early on with Aaron. Many figured that with his size he'd be best suited as a first baseman. But after seeing how well Aaron moved in the five-on-five football games and knowing what a fine pass receiver he was at Linden High, he saw no reason why he couldn't be an outfielder. The coach said if Aaron can run down a football then he can certainly run down a baseball. So an outfielder it was and he played both right field and center field at Fresno. And with his freshman year of 2011, his baseball career was about to begin in earnest.

CHAPTER TWO

FROM FRESNO TO THE MINOR LEAGUES

🏆

AARON QUICKLY WON A STARTING job with the Bulldogs, playing the outfield and hitting in the number-seven spot in the lineup. He was at his full height and weighed about 240 pounds. He started 49 of the team's 55 games and played very well. The Bulldogs had a strong team that went 17–7 in the Western Athletic Conference (WAC) and were 49–14 overall. The team was first in the WAC and won the postseason conference tournament before losing in the second round of the NCAA Regional Tournament. All in all, it was a successful season for Coach Batesole and the Bulldogs.

As for Aaron, he fit right in with his new teammates and made a large contribution to the ballclub. He batted an outstanding .358 with 67 hits in 187 at-bats. He had 12 doubles, a triple, two home runs and 30 runs batted in. He also showed he could run the bases with 11 steals in 12 tries, walked 25 times and struck out on 42 trips to the plate.

One thing, however, was obviously missing from what was a very successful freshman season. That was power. For a big, strapping guy who was very strong, just two home runs in 187 at-bats seems almost anemic. But Aaron's .358 batting average showed he was making contact. With some young players, even very strong ones like Aaron, it takes some time for the power to come. They have to refine their timing and their swings. Since he was just 19, no one was worried.

After the season, Aaron was named a Louisville Slugger Freshman All-American and was also the winner of the Western Athletic Conference Freshman of the Year award. A short time later, College Baseball Insider included him to the preseason honorable All-American team for the upcoming 2012 season. And when Aaron returned to Fresno for his sophomore year he had put on another 15 pounds of muscle and weighed in at 255 pounds.

The team had a good number of players return-ing from the previous season with Coach Batesole already deciding to move Aaron up to the third spot in the batting order, a place often reserved for a team's best hitter. Asked if he thought he'd get as many good pitches to hit batting third as opposed to lower in the lineup Aaron answered in a way that would carry over right into the big leagues. He would always talk about the team first.

"It's a team game," he responded. "As long as I've got good teammates around, we'll do well. There are not too many individual goals, just team goals for me. I'm going to just try to win the WAC and get on base for my teammates."

He also admitted that the loss in the NCAA regional tournament the year before still hurt. "There's a bad taste in everyone's mouth about it," he said, already exhibiting his great desire to win.

In some ways, the 2012 season was something of a letdown in that his numbers did not quite match up with those of his freshman season. In 58 games his batting average dropped to .308, still a good average but 50 points lower than his freshman year. Among his 62 hits were 14 doubles, two triples, and just four home runs. He drove home 27 runs, three fewer than the previous season. He again struck out 42 times but he also drew 48 walks. That showed he was being selective at the plate and the pitchers were working him carefully.

The team also didn't play as well, finishing 8–10 in the WAC and 31–28 overall. They made the NCAA playoffs, but were eliminated early. It might have been considered a disappointing season, but then something happened that July that once again put Aaron Judge on the map. He was invited to Omaha, Nebraska, to participate in the College Home Run Derby, site of the 2012 college World Series. Aaron was already playing summer ball in the Cape Cod League and had to fly from Massachusetts to Nebraska.

Given the fact that he had only hit four homers all year, Aaron was totally surprised by the invitation, saying, "Are you sure they want me out there?" But they did and he accepted, arranging his flight from Boston to Omaha.

Another collegian, Mason Katz, was also playing in Cape Cod and at the airport to take the same flight. He spotted Aaron and walked over to introduce himself.

"I'm just five-foot-nine," Katz recalled, "and when Aaron stood to shake my hand I remember looking straight up. We boarded the plane together and were still talking when Aaron hit his head on the doorway to the plane. I couldn't do that if I jumped. He was so tall."

Once in Omaha, other players gathering for the Derby were also awed by Aaron's size. Tyler Horan of Virginia Tech was another who introduced himself to Aaron, offering a handshake. "When I shook his hand, I felt like I was shaking an outfielder's mitt instead of somebody's hand," Horan said.

South Carolina's L.B. Dantzler, who was five-foot-ten, remarked that "as soon as you see [Aaron] you're like, 'Oh, he's the favorite; we're competing for second place."

During batting practice for the Derby, the other contestants were constantly watching Aaron in the batter's box. "Judge makes it look so easy," said Mason Katz. Another of the entrants, Daniel Aldrich of the College of Charleston, who had won the Derby the year before, remarked, "You don't see guys do what he can do. The ball comes off his bat different than everybody else."

While it was Aaron's size that intimidated his seven other contestants, they sure had to know about his home-run totals. He had just six in 113 games over his first two seasons, but they still apparently feared his presence. Then the contest began.

It was Mason Katz who took the early lead, hitting seven homers in the first round. Horan had five, while Aaron and Derek Fisher of Virginia hit four, allowing them to join Katz and Horan in the second round. That's when Katz ran his total to 12 while Aaron cracked four more, giving him eight, the same as Horan. All three now got ready for the final round where they would start from zero once again.

It was Tyler Horan who had the lead when Aaron stepped up for his final at-bats. There were some 22,400 fans in the ballpark, more than Aaron had ever played in front of before. He was finally down to his last out, still trailing by one home run. Then came the next pitch and he took that big, long swing of his and hit a drive out of the park to tie Horan. But he wasn't finished yet. He then slammed another to take the lead and actually win the contest. But the rules allowed him to finish up and he promptly belted a third straight homer.

"In college, on good nights, maybe you'd have 10,000 people [in the ballpark]," Aaron said. "Here after you hit one and two and three, [the crowd] gets a little excited and you can hear them, and you feed off that."

On the final pitch, Aaron fed off the crowd some more and smacked a long, fourth straight home run to win the contest going away.

"Judge makes it look so easy," Mason Katz said. "It takes every ounce of my five-foot-nine frame to get one out of the park. But he must have hit that last one 460 feet."

In a sense, Aaron's performance at the College Home Run Derby was the beginning of the Judge legend. Up to this point, the big guy was known as a fine college ballplayer, but not a super home-run threat. But with his size, strength and swing it had to come. And another part of Aaron Judge also showed itself at the Derby. He had great camaraderie with his fellow contestants as well as the fans. In between his swings, he was signing autographs for kids and others.

Coming into his junior year at Fresno, Aaron was beginning to be looked upon more favorably. He was chosen to three preseason All-American teams by Baseball America, Perfect Game, and by the National Collegiate Baseball Writers Association. The Bulldogs changed conferences, moving from the WAC to the Mountain West Conference where the coaches also made him as a preseason first-team choice. And Baseball America, in their evaluation of Aaron, had this to say:

> *"Judge's combination of size and athleticism is so unusual for a baseball player that the comparison scouts make most is to NBA star Blake Griffin (who stood six-foot-ten and weighed about 255 pounds). With his leverage and strength, Judge can hit tape-measure shots most players only can dream of. He homered just four times as a sophomore, but he went deep twice in one game in March and won the TD Ameritrade College Home Run Derby in July. As a right-handed hitter, Judge is still figuring himself out as a hitter, gets tied up by quality inside fastballs, and is overly selective at the plate. He draws walks but lets too many hittable pitches go by. Judge has solid speed and arm strength, and he'll probably move from center field in college to right field as a pro."*

It was quite an assessment, pretty much acknowledging that Aaron had the talent to become a
professional. That certainly didn't guarantee he'd
make it to the majors, but they apparently felt he
would sign with a big-league organization. Before
that happened, Aaron had to get ready for the 2013
season, his junior year at Fresno.

The Bulldogs, now in the Mountain West Conference,
were hoping to improve upon their 8–10 record from
the 2012 season in the WAC. But it wouldn't be easy.
Mountain West coaches rated the Bulldogs no better
than fourth in the conference. As for Aaron, he was
ready to go.

"I'm looking forward to just going out there and
playing some ball again," he said. "It's been a while, so
I'm just going out there and have some fun playing.
We want to go out and make a statement. We've got
a pretty young team but we've got a lot of talent.
Practice has been a little more intense these past few
weeks. We're just trying to get ready, get fired up for
that first game against Santa Barbara."

As for Coach Batesole, he was looking forward to
a big year from his biggest player. "Judge is playing
outstanding center field," the coach said. "He's an

outstanding base runner. Offensively he's going to hit in the middle of the order. We've got some guys this year I think can protect him well so that he's going to get some pitches. He isn't going to get 48 walks like he had last year. I think that's going to make his numbers increase just by that fact alone."

The coach was right about one thing. Aaron's numbers were up, but unfortunately the team didn't fare as well. The Bulldogs were just 14–16 in conference games and 23–33 overall, which eliminated them from NCAA tournament consideration. Yet Aaron was continuing to emerge as a star, drawing interest from major-league scouts at almost every game he played.

In 56 games, Aaron had 76 hits in 206 at-bats for an outstanding .369 batting average. Among his hits were 15 doubles, four triples, and 12 home runs. His power numbers were increasing. He also had 36 runs batted in, 12 stolen bases, walked just 35 times, down from the 48 the season before. The only negative was his 53 strikeouts. But, all in all, it was an outstanding season in which he was again named to the all-conference team. He had to be fully aware that the scouts were watching him and once again he would soon have to make a big decision.

During his three years at Fresno, Aaron hit .345 with 18 home runs and 93 runs batted in. He also had 41 doubles, seven triples, walked 108 times and struck out on 137 occasions. When you consider that he did that in 169 games, that's just a shade above the equivalent of a 162-game major-league season, so his totals stack up well. Only, now, the question again was, what next? He had another year of college eligibility but he also knew he was being scouted and that his goal was to play in major leagues. With the draft once again approaching, he had to play the wait-and-see game.

THE YANKEES COME CALLING

The drafting of high school and college players is never foolproof. Scouts and talent evaluators from major-league teams watch potential draftees carefully, not only noting their strengths and weaknesses, but also trying to project how they will develop over the next few years. That way they can advise their teams about those with the best chance to become valuable major leaguers.

What Aaron probably didn't know then was that one of the teams looking hard at him was the New York Yankees, baseball's most storied and successful franchise. These were the Yankees of Babe Ruth, Lou Gehrig, Joe DiMaggio, Mickey Mantle, Yogi Berra, Whitey Ford and, more recently, the likes of Don Mattingly, Derek Jeter, Mariano Rivera, and Andy Pettitte. The Yanks had won 27 World Series, by far the most in baseball. By 2013 the team was becoming old and stagnant, and they were looking for dynamic young players.

Scouting and evaluation of a young player is very complex. The player is under the microscope on many levels. Because the Yankees had three first-round draft picks in 2013, it was an opportunity to bring in a trio of good young players. Picking out future stars is far from an exact science, but the Yankee organization was hoping to get it right. Here's what they looked for and saw when it came to Aaron Judge.

There were a number of men involved in the process including area scout Troy Afenir, Vice President of Amateur Scouting Damon Oppenheimer, national crosschecker Brian Barber, and special assignment scout Jim Hendry. The four didn't have an easy job evaluating Aaron simply because there were so few players with which to compare him. They all had the same initial reaction. He looked more like a guy who would fit into the NFL or NBA draft because of his great size.

Jim Hendry, who had been a general manager and spent 39 years in baseball, put it this way when he saw Aaron for the first time.

"If you're going to be that big and become a good hitter, you've got to have a couple of things going for you. You've got to be a good athlete, which he is, and you've got to have really good makeup, because it's going to take a lot of work. You're going to have some holes and deficiencies to begin with, because you're such a big man. That's why the game hasn't had a lot more huge people."

But the Yankee brass could see quickly that Aaron wasn't just a big, lumbering slugger. The fact that he had played center field at Fresno pointed to his athleticism. He obviously moved very well or the coach wouldn't have put him out there. The scouts were also impressed with his batting-practice habits. He didn't just try to hit the ball as far as he could. He often concentrated on hitting the ball up the middle instead of trying to pull and lift everything.

"He hit no home runs in batting practice," Brian Barber said. "But he did hit about ten missiles off the center field wall, just low line drives. You knew the power was there."

The scouts knew that a guy with Aaron's bat speed and work ethic could learn how to produce more power once he was in a big-league organization. His athleticism was a plus. He could run and throw, and even steal a base. The one thing that still seemed risky was his great size. As Jim Hendry noted, there were only a small handful of players as big as Aaron who became great or even good major-league hitters.

"It was certainly not a lock that he was going to become an outstanding hitter," Hendry said. "It was going to take time and work. With big people, it always seems to take longer. A player that size has to be exceptional to learn how to become a polished hitter. When you're six-foot-seven it's not that easy to get to the ball low and away at your kneecaps."

That was something that would take plate discipline and hard work. Some never get there. A couple of fairly close comparisons could easily be Dave Kingman and Dave Winfield. Kingman was six-foot-six and weighed just 210 pounds, so he was thin for his size. But he could hit the ball a long way. Playing from 1971 to 1986, he hit 442 home runs. The problem was that he was one-dimensional. He wasn't a good defensive player, struck out often, and only had a .236 lifetime batting average. He also never stayed with one team very long, playing for a number of teams and always getting his share of home runs. But he didn't do the other things that make a complete, winning ballplayer.

One guy who did all that was Dave Winfield. He was also six-foot-six and weighed in the neighborhood of 220 pounds, probably gaining some weight as he got older. But Winfield, like Aaron Judge, was all athlete. He played baseball and basketball at the University of Minnesota and was considered such a superior athlete that he was not only drafted by Major League Baseball, but by teams in the NFL and NBA as well.

Winfield opted for baseball and played from 1973 to 1995, including a decade-long stint with the Yankees. He wound up with 465 homers, but also with 3,110 hits and a solid .283 lifetime batting average. In addition, he could play all three outfield positions, could run, and had a big-time throwing arm. In other words, he was a complete player and was rewarded after his retirement by being elected to the Baseball Hall of Fame.

As for contemporary players, the scouts looked at Miami's Giancarlo Stanton, who stood six-foot-six and weighed 245 pounds. From 2010 through 2013 Stanton already had 117 homers and looked like a coming star. He would fully validate that assessment in 2017 when he led the majors with 59 home runs.

So there certainly were some favorable comparisons to baseball's big men, and also, of course, big guys who didn't make the grade. But then again, drafting a prospect always has risks. There have been plenty of so-called "can't miss" prospects who never made it or became just marginal players. And there are also low draftees who come out of nowhere to become stars. But when all the reports were in and the organizational meetings concluded, the Yankees decided to act.

The Yanks initial pick in the opening round was in the 26th spot. With it, they chose collegiate third baseman Eric Jagielo. Six picks later it was the Yankees turn again and this time they went for the big guy, taking Aaron Judge at number 32 in the first round. If he signed this time, he'd be a New York Yankee.

There was one guy who was overjoyed by Aaron's selection. That was his college coach, Mike Batesole. He was so high on Aaron's abilities that he said, "I thought he should have been the first player taken in the whole draft."

But being chosen anywhere in the first round is an honor and, in today's game, worth a substantial bonus. On July 12, Aaron signed his first contract with the New York Yankees and with it came a bonus of $1.8 million dollars. That, of course, was just step one. Now he had to begin the arduous journey of becoming a major leaguer and hopefully taking his talents to Yankee Stadium.

THE MINOR LEAGUES

There are several levels in the minors that young players have to pass through, proving themselves each time as they go against older and better players all striving for the same thing—to make it to the majors. They usually begin in rookie ball, then go to Single-A, Double-A, and finally Triple-A. Those progressing the fastest can move up quickly and a special few can even jump from Double-A right to the majors.

In the low minors, players still have to take long bus rides of several hours or more to play games. Conditions and the stadiums are much better than they were years ago, but it's still a grind and not an easy life. But everyone has the same goal, to prove themselves, move up, and realize what is often a life-long dream.

Aaron had already completed the 2013 season at Fresno State, but after signing in July there was still time for more baseball, this time in the rookie league. Before he got to play in a single game he learned a frustrating reality about being a professional. Injuries can really derail you. While taking part in a base-running drill right after he came to camp he tore a quadriceps femoris muscle in his leg, and it would shelve him for the remainder of the season. He would have to wait until 2014 to begin his Yankees career.

But true to his positive outlook and tireless work ethic, he rehabbed the injury diligently and was ready to go when the spring of 2014 rolled around. His journey would begin at Charleston in the South Atlantic League. It was the lower of two levels of Single-A ball where most of the young players begin. But Aaron wasn't there very long. At about the halfway point in the season he was ready for his first promotion.

At Charleston, Aaron played in 65 games and came to bat 234 times. He hit .333 with 15 doubles, a pair of triples, nine home runs, and 45 runs batted in. He also walked 39 times and struck out on 59 occasions. His on-base percentage was an impressive .428. It was apparent he was ready for another challenge. So the organization moved him up to Tampa, the Yanks top Single-A team in the Florida State League. He would play the remainder of the season there.

As a player moves up the minor league chain, the competition becomes a bit tougher and that change was reflected in Aaron's numbers at Tampa. He played in 66 games, came to bat 233 times and hit .283, still solid but down 50 points from his average the first half at Charleston. He had nine doubles, two triples, eight home runs, and 33 RBIs. He used his good batting eye to walk 50 times but perhaps a bit alarmingly, his strikeouts rose to 72. He was still, clearly, a work in progress.

It was soon apparent, however, that the Yanks continued to have high hopes for him. After hitting .255 with four homers and 15 RBIs in 24 games in the Arizona Fall League, he learned he'd be opening the 2015 season with the Yanks Double-A farm team in Trenton, New Jersey. By this time, he weighed 275 pounds, yet this huge man still had his athletic ability, ran well, and played a very solid outfield. It could be said that his Yankee career was about to begin in earnest when spring training for the 2015 season began, and he was invited to the major-league camp for his first taste of real big-league action.

This is something teams do with their top prospects who are not quite ready for the majors. They invite them to the big-league camp and perhaps let them play a few games while absorbing the atmosphere and getting a feel for what it's like to be a major leaguer. Aaron also gave the Yanks a preview of what might be when in his first game against the Philadelphia Phillies on March 3, he belted a clutch ninth-inning homer to tie the game.

He had just twelve at-bats with the Yankees, getting three hits, a homer and three runs batted in. He also struck out four times. At that point, he and nine others were sent back to the minor-league camp to continue preparing for the season. When asked if his homer against the Phils was his most vivid memory of his time with the big club he gave a surprising answer.

"No. It was probably A-Rod's first home run this spring," Aaron said, referring to Alex Rodriguez. "He's a legend. Such a good hitter. And to be on this team, be in the dugout with him, to see it all happening, it was amazing. It's baseball."

In a sense, that marked the beginning of something that would become an Aaron Judge trait. Whenever he was asked to talk about himself he usually deflected to a teammate or, more often, the entire team. He was already a team-first guy, and it would stay that way.

Of the game played at the major-league level, Aaron said, "I notice, compared to the minor leagues, that there's not too many mistakes here. But you just have to find one and get it."

He also said that Yankee manager Joe Girardi told him to keep working hard at the minor-league camp and that his experience, though short with the big leaguers, gave him the confidence that he could play well with and against them.

"Now I just have to go out there and get better every day," he said.

So it was back to the Double-A Trenton Thunder to finish spring training and open the season. And he started it with a bang, hitting .314 in his first 34 games, and that included six home runs and 21 RBIs in 140 at-bats. The praise was beginning to come from friend and foe alike. Yankees General Manager Brian Cashman said that Aaron's makeup was "off the charts," adding, "If he keeps doing this then he is just going to force his way up. It's not an 'if,' it is a 'when.'"

Cashman was referring to the big club, the Yankees. And he wasn't the only one singing the praises of Aaron Judge. Bobby Meacham, who had once played for the Yankees but was now managing the Double-A Toronto Blue Jays affiliate, the New Hampshire Fisher Cats, said this about Aaron: "When you look at him, you say, 'Wow, that is what a big leaguer looks like.'"

Yankees legend and Hall of Famer Reggie Jackson was already comparing Aaron to big sluggers Dave Winfield, Willie Stargell, and Willie McCovey, all Hall of Famers. But Aaron was not about to fall victim to praise. It was nice to hear, but he knew he had to keep working if he wanted to make his mark in the majors. No one was about to hand it to him. That was something that had to be earned.

As had happened the season before in Single-A, Aaron played about half the season at Trenton before he was moved up again, this time to the Scranton/ Wilkes-Barre RailRiders, the Yanks Triple-A club in the International League. It happened after 61 games at Trenton in which Aaron batted a solid .284 with 12 homers and 44 RBIs. Now he was just a step away from the major leagues. It seemed to all that he was on a fast track.

Still, Aaron didn't have visions of glory at Yankee Stadium. He remained grounded and focused on what he had to do to improve.

"One thing I heard from my Double-A hitting coach was, 'Just be where your feet are,'" Aaron said. "Control what you can control. So right now I'm here in Scranton, trying to get better each day and trying to help the RailRiders win. [Praise] is nice to hear, but I really focus on what I can do on the field."

As happens often when a young player moves up to the next level, Aaron found he had to make adjustments at Triple-A. The pitchers were better and they were getting him out more often than when he was at Trenton. So with Yankee Stadium already on the radar, he suddenly found himself struggling at the plate.

Though he was working to get his bat going, Aaron was also forming bonds and friendships with some other highly-touted Yankee farmhands like first baseman Greg Bird, catcher Gary Sanchez and pitcher Luis Severino. It was the first time since the Derek Jeter, Andy Pettitte, Mariano Rivera, Jorge Posada days in the mid-1990s that the Yankees had such a group of potential young stars in their farm system.

At the same time, the big club had only won a single World Series since 2000, in 2009. The Yankees still had aging stars with huge contracts while many teams in the majors were younger and more athletic. The old Yankee model wasn't working, especially with the changing economics of the game. There was a time when the Yankees could outspend anyone for big-name free agents. Not so much anymore. Thus, there was more emphasis on the farm system and grooming young players.

The Yanks continued to be competitive, but were losing either in the wild-card game or early in the play-offs each year after 2009. In 2015, however, they were in first place behind two veterans having bounceback seasons—Alex Rodriguez and Mark Teixeira. A-Rod was coming off a suspension and Teix was coming back from an injury. With the trade deadline coming up in August, it was thought the Yankees would try to make a deal or two, getting players who might be able to help push them over the top. But, to do that, you've got to give up prospects. And the guy most teams would ask about immediately was Aaron Judge. Despite his struggles at Triple-A, he was still thought to have a huge upside.

But every time the Yanks were asked if they would consider trading Aaron, the answer was an emphatic no. He was a keeper.

CHAPTER THREE

THE MAJOR LEAGUES, AT LAST

🏆

DESPITE HIS STRUGGLES AT SCRANTON, Aaron was showing some improvement in key areas. In his first 22 games after moving up from Trenton, he seemed to have a better knowledge of the strike zone. His walk rate was up to 12.2 percent at Scranton from 8.6 percent at Trenton. And he had also cut back his 25 percent strikeout rate to 19.4 percent at Triple-A.

"I think it's just a matter of sticking to my approach," he said. "If I don't get my pitch, I'll take a walk, and

I know the guys behind me on our team are good enough to get me over or drive me in."

As always, he was thinking about the entire team, not just himself. And his overall approach at the plate was not to try to hit home runs. With his strength and power, he knew they would come. "If I square up on the ball, I may run into 25 or 30 home runs a year."

On the other side of the ball he was excelling as well. It didn't matter where he played in the outfield, he did a very good job.

"He does everything fundamentally the way you'd want," said his manager at Scranton, Dave Miley. "He always hits the cutoff man. He throws to the right base. He's made I don't know how many plays where he had to leave his feet. He gets great jumps. You put him in center, the only difference is he's the tallest center fielder I've seen."

The RailRiders hitting coach, Marcus Thames put it even more simply. "He's big, but he can move; he's athletic," Thames said. "I remember the first inning of a game when a ball was hit in the gap. He dove and caught it. I was like, 'Wow, he can do that.'"

But despite all the praise, Aaron's half season at Scranton continued to be a struggle. In 61 games, he hit just .224 in 228 at-bats. Included were eight home runs and 28 RBIs, but he struck out 74 times. He continued to be a highly rated prospect, but he had taken a small step back, his numbers at Triple-A not as impressive as his Double-A stats at Trenton the first half of the season. But combine his Trenton and Scranton numbers and he had a pretty good season, batting .255 with 20 homers and 72 RBIs. Nevertheless, he knew he had to prove himself at Triple-A before he'd have a chance to move up to the majors.

He continued to be optimistic while enjoying his time with the group of Yankee top prospects—Bird, Sanchez, Severino, and others.

"I've gotten to play with these guys the last two, three years, so we've gotten to be like brothers," Aaron said. "We hang out on and off the field basically all the time. So that would be pretty cool, wouldn't it? The next Core Eight? Core Nine?"

Aaron was referring to the famed Yankee Core Four, the young players who surfaced beginning in 1995 and helped the Yankees win four World Series in five years from 1996 to 2000. They were shortstop Derek Jeter, catcher Jorge Posada, and pitchers Andy Pettitte and Mariano Rivera. So, Aaron, like the other young players, was already well-versed in recent Yankees history and hoping he and his fellow top prospects could emerge to lead another winning dynasty.

The one young player in the group who got a taste of the majors in 2015 was Greg Bird. He was called up late in the season to play first base for the Yanks when Mark Teixeira suffered a season-ending injury. He adapted well, batting .261 with 11 homers and 31 RBIs in 46 games. He'd certainly tell his fellow prospects what it was like and make Aaron and the others hunger even more for the chance to pull on the Yankee pinstripes.

There was just one problem, something that had to be concerning for the Yankees. In the era of advanced statistics, when talent evaluators were looking at stats that no one had heard of years ago, it was noted that Aaron's BABIP has dropped at each step in the minors. (BABIP is batting average on balls in play. In other words, you don't count strikeouts or walks, just a player's batting average when he makes contact and puts the ball in play.) At Charleston, Aaron's BABIP was .408. Then at Tampa in high A ball it was .377. At Double-A Trenton it was down again to .345, but at Scranton it really took a dip to .289.

Some felt he simply did not make contact enough, though it was apparent that he hit the ball hard enough to have a solid batting average, that is, until he reached Scranton. There was also a feeling that his obvious raw power wasn't translating to game power, that he wasn't hitting enough home runs to offset his low on-base percentage. He also continued to strike out too much. Would it get even worse in the big leagues where the pitchers are better and more experienced? Though Aaron continued to have a positive attitude and optimistic outlook, to many the upcoming 2016 season would be pivotal. Now weighing more than 270 pounds, some wondered if Aaron was simply too big and tall to ever become a consistent big leaguer. There would be a big challenge just ahead.

THE CALL-UP

In a sense, Aaron was now under an ever-increasing microscope. Marcus Thames, the hitting coach at Scranton, felt some of Aaron's problems stemmed from his still learning to recognize breaking balls. Others echoed those words, saying he had to learn to lay off breaking balls, which will be thrown by mechanically sound pitchers who hide the ball well. But Aaron had been making adjustments all his baseball life. He knew his size, long arms, and long swing could lead to strikeouts. He had to keep his mechanics consistent and learn to repeat his swing. But pitch recognition is something else. It takes experience and sound judgment. He also knew he had to prove himself at Scranton before he could expect a call-up to New York.

Aaron played well in April. He didn't set the league on fire, but was holding his own. It still wasn't the improvement the Yankees were looking for, but he seemed more comfortable at Scranton than he had the second half of the previous season. Then came the month of May and suddenly the big guy couldn't do anything right. He began struggling at the plate, striking out, not hitting a lick and certainly not looking anything like someone the Yankees would be calling up to the big club any time soon. In fact, in some ways he seemed to be playing himself right back to Double-A ball. He hit an anemic .183 in the month of May, and that just wouldn't cut it.

By June 3, Aaron's overall batting average stood at just .221 and he had looked lost at the plate the entire month of May. But then something happened. Aaron's bat not only came alive, it ignited and was on fire. He began hitting the ball hard as well as hitting for power, and carrying the RailRiders on the broad back.

His strong hitting continued for the entire month and certainly caught the attention of the Yankees brass back in New York. Just look at the numbers.

For the month of June, Aaron batted .343 while leading the International League with nine home runs, 30 runs scored and a .477 on-base percentage. He also drove in 25 runs, had 16 extra base hits and a .686 slugging percentage. All impressive numbers. In addition, he reached base in 25 of the 28 games he played and had 11 games with more than one hit. His hot streak led the RailRiders to a 19–10 record for the month, enabling them to open up a two-and-a-half-game lead in the league's North Division.

Aaron's hot streak raised his season's average from .221 to .270. He was named the International League's Player of the Month and also the Batter of the Week for June 20–26. In addition, he was voted a starting outfielder for the league's All-Star game, set for July 13. His nine homers in June gave him 16 for the year, tied for the league lead.

Once again there were calls for the Yankees to bring Aaron up to the big club. But one hot month doesn't tell a story. When asked about a possible call-up, Yankees manager Joe Girardi said this about Aaron:

"Those really aren't my decisions, I'm not watching [Aaron] every day. Obviously our minor league people are trying to finish this kid off so if and when he gets here, he's here to stay. He's gotten really hot, but you also go through down periods. We're seeing improvement, which I think is really positive. We're seeing things we didn't necessarily see last year."

In a sense, the time was right for some of the Yanks' top prospects to get called up. Greg Bird had shown he was major-league ready the year before, when he replaced an injured Teixiera. Unfortunately, a shoulder injury that flared up in the spring of 2016 necessitated surgery and Bird would miss the entire 2016 season. But it was the overall situation with the Yankees that gave Aaron and some others hope they would get the call soon.

There was no doubt that the Yanks were baseball's most successful franchise, proof being in their 27 World Championships, the most of any franchise by far. But things were not so good in the few years leading up to the 2016 season. Led by the original Core Four along with some outstanding veterans, the team won four World Series in five years from 1996 to 2000. They reached the series again in 2001 and 2003, but were defeated. Still, that team represented the latest Yankee dynasty, of which there had been several over the years beginning in the days of Babe Ruth in the 1920s.

The team stayed in contention throughout the decade and finally won another championship in 2009. But they did it the old Yankee way, importing high-priced veteran stars and handing out long-term contracts. To win in 2009 they dipped into the free-agent market for pitchers CC Sabathia and A.J. Burnett as well as first baseman Mark Teixeira to join the Jeter–Posada–Rivera–Pettitte quartet, now an aging Core Four, as well as Alex Rodriguez, who came to the team in 2004.

While the Yanks remained in contention the next couple of years, the team was aging at a time when many other clubs were going to more young and athletic players. They missed the playoffs completely in 2013 and 2014, made it to the wild-card in 2015 only to be beaten in the one-game wild-card playoff game by Houston. Coming into 2016 there were many questions, especially with the high-priced, aging players now past their primes and the Core Four all retired. The team finally had some outstanding prospects at Scranton, including Aaron, Gary Sanchez, Luis Severino, and the injured Greg Bird. So speculation about calling up a couple of the youngsters was increasing, especially with Teixeira and Sabathia injured and Alex Rodriguez failing badly.

At the July 31, trade deadline, the Yankees finally changed the way they frequently did business. General Manager Brian Cashman traded his two top relief pitchers, Aroldis Chapman and Andrew Miller, as well as veteran Carlos Beltran for a basketful of young prospects. Chapman and Miller would both help their new teams, the Cubs and Indians respectively, to reach the World Series, but the highly rated young prospects the Yankees received from all three traded players quickly made their farm system one of the best in the majors.

Finally, it was time to start looking at the youngsters. Luis Severino along with Greg Bird had been called up late in the 2015 season. Severino pitched well as a starter in his short audition, but faltered badly the beginning of 2016. He was sent down and came back late in the season to pitch well out of the bullpen. But the Yanks still weren't sure what his future would be. Then on August 2, Gary Sanchez was called up. Like Aaron, Sanchez was a power hitter and he soon took the number-one catching job away from vet Brian McCann. He began hitting home runs and showing a cannon for an arm behind the plate.

Sanchez, at age 23, played in 53 games the rest of the way, hitting 20 home runs, driving in 42 and finishing with a .299 batting average. It appeared the Yankees had their catcher of the future as well as a potential superstar. Maybe it was Sanchez's immediate success that helped the Yankees decide to look at more of their youngsters. With the team heading for another season of not making the playoffs, the Yankee brass decided to make a daring move. They released long time star Alex Rodriguez, even though he was under contract through 2017. As great as A-Rod had been (He finished his career with 696 home runs.) the team felt it couldn't keep a struggling veteran any longer with youngsters at Scranton chomping at the bit.

On the same day A-Rod's release was announced, the Yankees summoned Aaron Judge to the major leagues. A Brett Gardner injury allowed a second call-up so the Yanks also tabbed a young first baseman/outfielder, Tyler Austin. With Sanchez already there and Judge and Austin joining him, the new group already had a nickname, the Baby Bombers, a play on the longtime team nickname, the Bronx Bombers.

A call-up isn't always a simple thing. Depending where the Triple-A club is located, a young player sometimes has to travel a long distance quickly. In Aaron's case, his parents were visiting him in Scranton and the three were eating dinner at a local restaurant when Scranton manager Al Pedrique suddenly appeared with the news that the Yankees were calling Aaron up and wanted him at Yankee Stadium for the game the following afternoon.

Pennsylvania isn't that far from New York, but it was almost midnight when Aaron got the news. Judge had played a game that night, so he and his parents were having a late dinner. They finished quickly, took Aaron so he could pack, then drove all night to New York City, arriving at 6:30 a.m. Aaron had to be ready to play a game shortly after 1:00 p.m.

That first big-league game turned out to be special in several ways. The Yanks were playing the Tampa Bay Rays, but before the game began Aaron got a taste of the great Yankees tradition. The ballclub had a ceremony to honor the 1996 championship team with many of the players from that squad in attendance. Imagine a young player like Aaron sitting in the dugout and watching Derek Jeter run out to shortstop and Mariano Rivera jog in from the bullpen. It had to be exciting, but was just a prelude to the excitement to come.

Aaron started the game in right field, with fellow call-up Tyler Austin at first. In the bottom of the second inning, Austin prepared to walk up for his first big-league at-bat. Aaron was also out of the dugout moving into the on-deck circle.

"Do your thing, T," was what Aaron said to his teammate.

And Austin did, smacking a line drive just inside the right-field foul pole and into the first row of seats for a home run. Not many players homer on their first big-league at-bat, so Aaron knew it was special as he watched Austin circle the bases.

"I was ecstatic on deck," Aaron said. "I was like, 'Oh man, I just got to make contact now.' What a day."

Aaron walked slowly to the plate as the crowd cheered, many in awe of Aaron's six-foot-seven, 275-pound frame. He got in the batter's box and looked for his pitch. He took the first three and on the fourth took that big long swing. The crack of the bat was unmistakable and the ball soared majestically high toward center field. It landed over the tinted glass windows beyond the center field wall some 446 feet from home plate. It was a mammoth blast and Aaron became just the third player at the new Yankee Stadium to reach that spot.

The back-to-back homers by the rookies marked the first time in baseball history that teammates had hit home runs in their first at-bats in the same game. Both Aaron and Austin each had another hit before the game ended and the Yanks won it, 8–4. It was the Yanks' fourth straight win, but it only brought their record to 60–56 for the year. With that kind of season, it was no surprise that the team wanted to look at its young prospects.

"The roster has been changing a lot," General Manager Brian Cashman said, before the game. "Today is a new day, but it's been a new day quite often lately, to be honest. We've had a lot of changes with a lot of quality people that we've said goodbye to, and a lot of quality people we've been saying hello to."

But would the hello to Aaron Judge last? He had certainly impressed in his big-league debut, and there was no doubt the Yankees planned to play him every day to see just how far he had come. It was quickly apparent that Aaron was more than a big, lumbering slugger. He was an athlete who moved well in the outfield, could run the bases, and quickly showed a very strong throwing arm. In the eyes of most, including the fans, they viewed him as a guy who was going to hit a lot of home runs. The shot he hit in his first big-league at-bat has served as a preview, and also a teaser. He had wound up his season at Scranton with 19 home runs, 65 RBIs and a .270 batting average in 93 games. But now none of that mattered.

Aaron did play every day but there was no explosion of home runs. With his long swing, strikeouts had to be expected. But not this many. Aaron wasn't getting a lot of hits, and he was walking back to the dugout too often. In fact, he was striking out in nearly half his at-bats, and that's too much. The highlights were few and far between, but when he did hit a home run, it almost always traveled a long way. By mid-September Aaron was struggling along with just a .179 batting average and only four home runs in 84 at-bats to go along with just 10 RBIs in 27 games. He had also struck out 42 times. That's when it was announced that he had to go on the disabled list with a strained oblique muscle. His season was over.

Despite the injury and his less-than-successful debut, Aaron tried to stay upbeat and look at the bright side. It was something he had always done. Though he hated to miss the rest of the season with an injury, he was still like a wide-eyed kid in a candy store.

"It was a dream come true," he said "That was probably the best year in baseball I've ever had. Anytime you get called up to the big leagues, it's a good thing. So for me it was like a practice test, where coming into this year you've had a chance to see what the league's about, get used to the travel, get used to the stadiums and playing in from of 40,000 people. I'm excited I got that opportunity. I'm just ready to get going."

But there was still no guarantee that Aaron would be back with the Yankees in 2017 or be returned to Scranton for more seasoning. The potential was certainly there, but with potential results have to follow. Potential doesn't win baseball games. Manager Joe Girardi was just one person who wasn't convinced that Aaron was ready for prime time.

"The strikeouts are a concern," the manager said. "To me, it's cutting down on the strikeouts and, if he does that, I think he's going to have success at this level. The hard part is not getting here. The hard part is sticking. And as people adjust to you, you have to make adjustments as a ballplayer."

Adjustments were something Aaron had been making for a long time. "It was the same thing last year," he said. "I got a little taste of Triple-A and got used to it and same thing here. Got a couple of games up here and saw what it's like. It'll help me prepare coming in here. I'll know what's going on, how the league is, and just kind of be prepared."

What surprised many of the veterans was how Aaron never changed, even when he was struggling and striking out way too much. Third baseman Chase Headley spoke for many when he said, "You never saw a change in him. You wouldn't know what his batting average was by his mood, which is not always the case. He was confident and always involved and not shut off. I was impressed the way he handled himself."

Bench coach Rob Thomson agreed. "He struck out in half his at-bats and never changed. He walked into the clubhouse the same every day, his head up, his chest out, like 'let's go.'"

The only disappointment for Aaron was that the oblique injury caused him to miss the final weeks of the season. He felt the learning experience was that important to the point that each game counted.

"You want to try to suck up as much as you can, especially with the guys we've got in this clubhouse," he said. "Having [Mark] Teixeira here in his last year, you try to pick his brain a little bit. I got a lot of good information in the weeks I was here. I'll take it into the off-season and just get ready for next year. Everyone's got to earn their spot."

CHAPTER FOUR

THE 2017 SEASON BEGINS

🏆

WHILE THE YANKEES FARM SYSTEM had been rebuilt and was now loaded with a group of highly rated young prospects, the outlook for 2017 wasn't that bright. Prospects, no matter how highly rated, are just prospects until they prove themselves at the major-league level. That's where Aaron Judge was when the Yankees reported to spring training in February. He had shown glimpses of his enormous power and potential, but glimpses aren't enough. If he didn't prove himself in the spring, he knew he'd be right back in Scranton when the season began.

Young Gary Sanchez had established himself as the new catcher with vet Brian McCann traded to Houston. Greg Bird was expected to return from his shoulder injury and play first base. The Yankees did have a young double-play combination with Starlin Castro at second and the improving Didi Gregorius at short. Vet Chase Headley was expected to man third base, while veterans Brett Gardner and Jacoby Ellsbury would be in left and center respectively. As soon as spring training began Manager Girardi said that Aaron Judge and Aaron Hicks, who had come over from Minnesota the season before, would fight it out in the spring for the right field job.

The big question was the pitching staff. There were worries about CC Sabathia's age and his balky knee, Masahiro Tanaka's elbow, whether young Luis Severino could succeed as a starter after an up-and-down 2016, and if the erratic Michael Pineda would be good or bad—or a little of both. The fifth spot was still open. The bullpen looked solid. The team had re-signed closer Aroldis Chapman after trading him to the Cubs for top prospects the season before. And they still had Dellin Betances, one of the top relievers in the league. But, all in all, most preseason predictions were that the Yankees would be at least a .500 team, but how much better? No one knew.

As the preseason games began GM Cashman pulled no punches when he talked about the right field competition between the two Aarons, Judge and Hicks. He said if Judge didn't win the regular job he would probably be sent back to Scranton because he had minor-league options left and the Yankees would want him to play every day. So the pressure was on.

"You just never want to get comfortable," Aaron said. "You just want to keep going in there and have the fire that you're trying to prove a point and win a job. And I feel like that's everybody going into camp. They're going in there trying to win a job. My first spring training, I was trying to take a job. It's a good attitude to have."

Just to make sure he wouldn't become too comfortable, Aaron put a succinct note on his iPhone. It simply read ".179," his batting average during his 2016 late-season call-up. He said he would look at it every day as a reminder to him that .179 just wouldn't cut it. To make the team and win a starting job, he'd have to hit much better than that.

Aaron came into camp at about 280 pounds, which is absolutely huge for a position player, especially an outfielder. The added weight was muscle and it didn't affect his athletic ability or his speed. With his huge potential, why were so many skeptical of him becoming a consistent, everyday player and not a guy who would strike out a lot and hit an occasional tape-measure home run? The answer again was in his size.

GM Cashman explained that going by the new analytics, computer generated statistics about every facet of the game and its players, Aaron was a risky draft choice. "From an analytics standpoint, you try to make safe bets," Cashman said, "and Judge coming out of college was six-foot-seven, and he had a lot of strikeouts, and from a historical standpoint in this game, being six-foot-seven is obviously a detriment."

It was the same reason people had questioned Aaron before. Players that tall and with long arms, most always have long swings and can get jammed up by inside pitches, thus a lot of strikeouts. And the game's history also showed that there were only 12 players who were six-foot-six or taller who had made more than 1,000 plate appearances in big-league history. Some, like Dave Winfield, were Hall of Fame successful. But with Aaron there were those 42 strikeouts in 84 at-bats at the end of the 2016 season. So it would be fully up to him to prove himself.

Spring training is a way to get the team in shape and see what it looks like. For the veterans, it's a matter of getting back into the swing of things, which means at-bats for the hitters and innings for the pitchers. It's also a way to give minor leaguers a taste of the majors, as was the case with Aaron in 2015. And, finally, it can be a way to determine which of two players will win a starting job, in this instance the two Aarons, Judge and Hicks.

Aaron Hicks had come to the Yanks in a trade the season before and had not played well. But the team felt he had a lot of potential and a shot to win a regular job. Hicks played well in the spring, showing the ballclub more of his total talent. He was a fine outfielder who could play all three outfield positions. He had great speed, a fine throwing arm, and was a switch hitter with some power. The team was very high on him and he didn't disappoint. He had a solid spring, hitting .268 in 56 at-bats with three homers and seven RBIs. It would be easy to make a case that he earned the job. Except for one thing. Aaron Judge suddenly looked like a whole different player, especially at the plate.

He seemed to be showing more plate discipline, thus cutting down on his strikeouts. Like Hicks, Judge had three homers and seven RBIs. But he was proving to be much more than a home-run hitter. In 63 at-bats Aaron had 21 hits and a .333 batting average. No longer was he striking out half the time, as he had done in his 2016 cameo. In the spring he fanned just 15 times. And he continued to be no slouch in the outfield, showing surprising speed for a man his size as well as a fine throwing arm. Though the competition was close, just before the start of the regular season Aaron Judge was named the starter. He wouldn't be returning to Scranton unless his fine spring didn't carry over to the season. Aaron Hicks also stayed with the team as the fourth outfielder.

That wasn't all. Greg Bird, returning after missing the 2016 season to shoulder surgery was perhaps the best hitter in the majors in spring training. The lefty-swinging first baseman hit a robust .451 with eight homers and 15 RBIs in 23 games, while catcher Sanchez had a .373 spring average with five home runs and 16 ribbies in just 19 games. That gave the Yankees a trio of young players who all had the potential to be impact power hitters.

The Yankees opened the 2017 season on April 2 in Tampa, and lost to the Rays, 7–3, with Masahiro Tanaka taking the defeat. The team was missing shortstop Didi Gregorius who had strained a shoulder playing in the World Baseball Classic, held before the Major League season, and could be out a month. While utility man Ronald Torreyes took his place,

Gregorius was expected to be a big part of the offense while anchoring the infield. The team won the next day, 5–0, behind CC Sabathia, but then promptly lost three straight and were suddenly at 1–4. Every team likes to get off to a fast start, but for the Yankees, this certainly wasn't it.

In that third straight loss, the Yanks also suffered a tough blow. Catcher Gary Sanchez took a big cut and fouled a ball off. Right after the swing it was apparent that Sanchez had hurt his right arm. He was removed from the game and later diagnosed with a right biceps strain. It was estimated that he could miss a month. With Gregorius also out, there were now two regulars down. At the same time, Greg Bird was not looking like the same hitter he had been in the spring. Bird had fouled a ball off his ankle late in spring training, and, while he said he was fine, some felt it was affecting his swing.

Injuries, of course, are something every team has to deal with, and it's up to the healthy players to pick up the slack. Aaron was looking good at the plate in those first five games hitting well in the early going, but his output was confined to singles and doubles. He still hadn't hit one out. Now, with Sanchez on the shelf and Bird not hitting, the Yankees needed his power bat more than ever. Then, in game number six, at Camden Yards in Baltimore, Judge delivered, hitting his first home run in the eighth inning of a 7–3 Yankees come-from-behind win.

A day later, back at the Stadium against Tampa, he hit a bases-empty homer in the fourth inning to give his team a 1–0 lead in what turned into an 8–1 victory behind Michael Pineda. Two homers in two days was a start, and when he hit a two-run shot two days later in yet another win over Tampa, he began to open some eyes. Home run number three was a shot, going an estimated 435 feet. He had now hit three dingers in four days, and still no one was quite prepared for what was about to come. In the ensuing weeks, Aaron Judge, who almost didn't make the team out of spring training, was about to become the most talked-about player in the sport and, in the eyes of many, the new face of Major League Baseball.

Between the opening of the season on April 2, through May 3, Aaron hit 13 home runs to lead the major leagues. He had been on a real tear, hitting six in the past six games and 10 in the past 14. But that wasn't all; he also had a .330 batting average, showing his increased plate discipline and ability to go with the pitch. The right-handed hitting Judge was taking outside pitches to right field, showing he wasn't pull happy, and when he wasn't putting the ball over the wall he was getting singles and doubles all over the park. Even if the Yanks expected the power, it was the batting average that really surprised them. Aaron looked like a completely different player from his 2016 call-up. In fact, he was looking like an all-star.

And his homers weren't just homers. The ESPN home run tracker had only two of his 13 home runs classified as just getting there. Six of them were blasts of 425 feet or more, most in the majors traveling that distance. One of baseball's new stats was exit velocity, measuring the speed at which the ball comes off the bat. Aaron had already set a record for exit velocity when one of his homers was measured as leaving the bat at 119.4 miles per hour. The old record of 119.2 mph was set by the Marlins' Giancarlo Stanton.

In addition, no rookie before him had ever hit 13 homers in the first 25 games of a season, and that led to him being named American League Rookie of the Month. The Yankees now had a surprising 17–9 record and a one-game lead in the American League's Eastern Division. ESPN's Keith Law, who had been tracking Aaron's season, gave this analysis of his amazing improvement at the plate:

"He has become more disciplined, more selective, and is forcing pitchers to be even more precise. I still think

there are ways to pitch Judge, but if you miss, this is
what happens. I really do believe he is going to be a star
for a long time because of his ability to make that adjust-
ment to control the strike zone enough where pitchers
have very little margin for error."

Fans, the media, and players alike were noticing something else, as well. In an era where more players in all sports often showboat and try to attract attention to themselves, Aaron Judge was the exception. When he hit one of his moonshot home runs, there was no posing at the plate watching the ball soar into the seats; no flipping the bat high in the air, no chest pounding or pointing. He would simply hit the ball, start running hard to first, then jog around the bases without smiling or gloating. And in his interviews, which were now many, he never spoke about himself. Even when asked directly about his hot streak, he'd always deflect the question to the team and the importance of winning. With Aaron, it was always team first, no matter what.

Fans at Yankee Stadium and even at the other ballparks where the team played were coming out early just to watch Aaron take batting practice. The sight of a six-foot-seven, 282-pound giant hitting long soaring drives even in batting practice had become a huge attraction. Stories were being written about him everywhere and his team jersey was already the biggest seller in baseball.

By the end of May, his home-run pace had slowed slightly. But he was still leading the league with 17 and the team finished the month with a 30–20 mark, giving them a two-game lead in the division. With the first early returns in the All-Star Game voting being tallied, Aaron had the third most votes in the majors among outfielders, trailing only young superstars Bryce Harper of Washington and Mike Trout of the Angels. He even seemed somewhat awed by his success and the attention it had garnered.

"It's pretty surreal," he said. "I'm living the dream. I'm getting to play a game, a kid's game, a game I've played since I was a little kid playing T-ball. I enjoy every day I come to the ballpark. We've got a good team here and I'm blessed to be in this situation."

Yankee second sacker Starlin Castro spoke for many of his teammates when he said of Aaron, "A guy that's 285 and moves like a shortstop. A great person, too, and I think the fans love that. He's the face of baseball, like [Mike] Trout and those guys."

The Yankees also knew what they had in Aaron, both as a player setting records and also someone they could promote. Since so much of sports today is about merchandising, there were Aaron Judge items for sale all over Yankee Stadium and online. The Yankees created The Judge's Chambers, a special rooting section out in right field named in honor of the big rookie. It was something that had never been done before.

A group of 18 seats framed by wood paneling and covering three rows was set up to look like a jury box and could seat 18 fans. Those lucky enough to sit there were given black judicial robes to wear with a Yankees logo on the front and Aaron's number 99 on the back. A cross-section of fans was chosen to sit there at each game with the plan to branch out for community groups, charitable organizations, Little Leaguers, schools, hospital workers, and others. And the slogan used was "All rise," something that is said in courtrooms when the judge enters.

Asked where the "All rise" slogan came from, Aaron said, "It just showed up one day. I had no part of that. I got a job to do on the field, so I think the behind-the-scenes people took care of that one. The fans like it. It kind of fits, so I just kind of rolled with it."

At the same time, Aaron said he found the whole Judge's Chambers concept a bit humbling to him. "I was shocked," he said, "you know, surprised. I think it's pretty cool. When you come to a game, it's supposed to be fun for the players and the fans. So I think it turned out great."

There would even be a very special day for the Judge's Chambers in late August when Sonia Sotomayor, an Associate Justice of the Supreme Court as well as a longtime Yankees fan, watched the game from there. Like the others in those special seats, Justice Sotomayor donned the judge's robe with the Yankees logo and held the foam gavel with ALL RISE printed on it.

"My life has changed so much, and we have a new Yankee Stadium," she said. "But the spirit of the Yankees is still in the house. And it's very moving for me and important to me that the comfort that [the Yankees] gave me most of my life—in watching them most of the time win—continues. And you can tell I'm a shrill of a fan."

After the game that day, both Aaron and Gary Sanchez had the chance to meet Justice Sotomayor. Both players were overjoyed at meeting her.

"Pretty cool experience," Aaron said. "She's from the Bronx, big Yankee fan." He also said that Justice Sotomayor told them that it was "great to meet you guys.

Just keep doing what you guys are doing. It's fun to watch. You guys are doing something special here."

While the Yanks were still in first place, there were some changes with the team. Sanchez and Gregorius were back and starting to make major contributions. But Bird was sent back down to Scranton after getting just six hits in his first 60 at-bats, a .100 average. At Scranton he would continue to insist there was a problem with his ankle. It took until July to solve the mystery when he had a small bone removed from his foot in the ankle area. He hoped he would make it back before the season ended. The team also lost center fielder Jacoby Ellsbury to a concussion. He received it when it hit the wall making a great catch. He would be out for a month. His place was taken by Aaron Hicks who was also playing very well and who had continued to produce after his fine spring.

ON TO THE ALL-STAR BREAK

Then when June rolled around, Aaron's home-run bat began tuning up again. The Yanks continued to hold on to first place in the division, and in mid-month Aaron went on another of his patented tears. He hit one on June 2, cooled off for a week and then exploded. He would hit another on the 10th, then two more the next day and yet another the day after that. Then he hit four more between June 20 and June 28. Once again, he was the talk of baseball.

He really made headlines on June 11, against the Orioles at Yankee Stadium. He came up in the bottom of the sixth inning against Orioles right-hander Logan Verrett and caught a fastball just right. The ball soared high and deep to left-center field landing way back in the stands. Statcast, the new method of tracking homers, measured the drive at 496 feet, making it the longest home run since they began keeping the stat in 2009. Later in the same game he hit a two-run shot to right field that had Manager Girardi gushing.

"He hit a line drive to right field," Girardi said. "It was just a line drive. Most guys, they're hoping it gets in the gap. [Aaron's] just went out. I mean, his power is incredible."

As for Aaron, it seemed as if nothing had gone to his head. He remained the same humble, team-first guy he had always been. He knew he'd have questions thrown at him after the game about his mammoth home run and he quickly deflected it to the team. "To be honest, it means nothing," he said. "I'm just glad we came away with a win." Then he spoke about how good the Yankees pitchers had been.

And win they did that day, taking the game, 14–3, which brought their record to 37–23. At that point in the season Aaron was leading the AL with 21 homers and 41 runs batted in, and also with a .344 batting average. If the season had ended that day, he would have won the Triple Crown of hitting. His 21 home runs were already the most by a Yankee player under the age of 26 before All-Star weekend since Roger Maris in 1960.

Aaron's home-run barrage continued to the end of the month. His home run on June 28, gave him 27 for the season. He was still hitting over .300 and driving in runs. There was already talk in the air about him perhaps hitting 60 home runs and winning both the Rookie of the Year and Most Valuable Player Awards at season's end. He was also now the leading vote getter for the All-Star Game, which would be played in mid-July. At the same time, the Yanks were 43–35 and still held a two-game lead in the division.

In many ways, Aaron had been really carrying the team offensively. Now, however, he was getting strong support from catcher Sanchez, who had found his power stroke, and shortstop Gregorius, who was having his finest season. But there were problems, as well. Matt Holliday, a 37-year-old former all-star, while in the National League with a lifetime batting average over .300, was signed before the season to serve as the primary designated hitter. Holliday batted cleanup the first couple of months of the season and was having a terrific year, hitting his share of homers and driving in runs. He also served as a mentor to Aaron, often standing side-by-side with him in the dugout and talking baseball. In late June, he was diagnosed with a viral infection that was sapping his strength. He had to go on the disabled list, and shortly after he returned in late July, he suffered a lumbar strain that put him right back on the DL.

That wasn't all. Second baseman Starlin Castro was having hamstring problems and had two DL stints that set him back. And righty Michael Pineda, counted on for a bounce back season, was 8–4 in early July when he hurt his elbow. The injury was more serious than first thought when it was found he needed ligament-replacement surgery and would be lost for the season. But through it all, Aaron's great play and home-run prowess was keeping the Yanks in the playoff race.

The growing Judge legend continued. On July 4, the Yankees lost a 4–1 game to the Blue Jays at the Stadium. The one run was another mammoth blast by Aaron that smashed off a metal sign deep in left center field and left a large dent in the sign. The ball traveled an estimated 453 feet. A day later he hit yet another, and two days after that, on July 7, blasted one that traveled 432 feet. That gave him 30 home runs for the season and the sky seemed the limit. That home run also enabled him to break an 81-year-old Yankees rookie record, topping the great Joe DiMaggio's mark of 29, set way back in 1936. More hoopla for the big guy. He had done in half a season what took DiMag an entire season to accomplish.

There was just one problem. The Yankees lost all three games, the first two to Toronto and the third to Milwaukee. The team wasn't playing well. They had lost six of their last eight. With their record now at 44–40, they had dropped to four-and-a-half games behind the division-leading Red Sox. They split their final two games before the All-Star break, were at 45–41, but managed to pick up a game on the Sox. Pitching was part of the problem with Masahiro Tanaka having an up-and-down year and not pitching like an ace. Pineda had been lost to elbow surgery and there were even some problems in their vaunted bullpen.

In addition, Aaron Hicks, who had played very well in Ellsbury's absence, went on the DL with an oblique strain on June 26. On July 1, the Yanks called up one of their top prospects, outfielder Clint Frazier, who made an immediate impact with a homer in his first game. So it continued to be a balancing act with the injured players.

Though the Yanks had played 86 games, the All-Star break was the symbolic end to the first half of the season. The good news was that Aaron Judge was the starting right fielder for the American League and had also agreed to participate in the much-anticipated Home Run Derby, held the day before the game. That was something every baseball fan in the country wanted to see.

made an immediate impact with a homer in his first game. So it continued to be a balancing act with the injured players.

Though the Yanks had played 58 games, the All-Star break was the symbolic end to the first half of the season. The good news was that Aaron Judge was the starting right fielder for the American League and had also agreed to participate in the much-anticipated Home Run Derby, held the day before the game. That was something every baseball fan in the country wanted to see.

CHAPTER FIVE

THE HOME RUN DERBY AND THEN THE SLUMP

♛

AARON CAME INTO THE ALL-STAR break hitting .329 with 30 home runs and 66 runs batted in. He continued to be the talk of baseball and, in the first half, its best player. Chris Archer, the Tampa Bay Rays top pitcher was one of many who said Aaron was the face of baseball in 2017.

"First of all, he plays in New York, and second he's a presence," Archer explained. "I mean, he's six-foot-seven, 280, and he's doing what he's doing, so at this particular moment, it's him. I'd say, in the past [Mike]

Trout, definitely. [Bryce] Harper, definitely. But now? Aaron Judge.

"And he's a good person. You can tell he's very humble and keeps his nose clean. People say this, and he has a lot more to accomplish, but he may be the second coming of Derek Jeter."

Jeter, of course, was the Yankees star shortstop and captain whose 20-year career ended in 2014. He was a leader who, like Aaron, played the game the right way. He gave everything for the team without showboating and played hard every game of his career.

Now Aaron was in Miami for his first All-Star Game. But first was the Home Run Derby. The defending champion was Giancarlo Stanton of the home town Marlins. Stanton was six-foot-six and 245 pounds, not as big as Aaron, but still a very tall and extremely strong player who had found success in the big leagues and, before Aaron came along, the guy who hit the longest homers in the game. It wasn't surprising that Aaron had taken notice of him.

"[Stanton] was the big guy that was having success in the big leagues," Aaron said, admitting he had studied videos of Stanton. "I was like, 'What's this guy doing that I can incorporate in my swing?' He uses his legs well, his barrel stays through the zone for a long time, so he's able to barrel up a lot of balls...and he's an athlete out there, too."

Stanton, who was constantly being asked questions about Aaron, said he was looking forward to meeting him. "Hopefully, he has to answer as many questions about me as I do about him," Stanton said.

Now it was time for the Derby. Everyone was hoping for an Aaron Judge–Giancarlo Stanton matchup in the final round. There were eight contestants in all. Aaron was joined by teammate Gary Sanchez along with Minnesota's Miguel Sano and Kansas City's Mike Moustakas to represent the American League. Stanton also had a teammate in the Derby, Justin Bour. They were joined by the LA Dodgers rookie slugger, Cody Bellinger and Colorado's Charlie Blackmon to round out the National League field.

The rules for the 2017 Derby allowed each player four minutes to hit as many home runs as he could against a pitcher of his own choosing. The pitcher can be a coach or even a relative. Robinson Cano once won it with his father throwing to him. In the first round and semifinals, players are allowed one 45-second time out. Once the second player in a round passes the total of the first player, the round ends. There's no need to see how many more home runs the second player can hit. If a player hit two home runs of 440 feet or better, he would earn a bonus of 90 seconds to hit more home runs if he needed it.

In the opening round, Sano defeated Moustakas, 11–10. Then came the Yanks Gary Sanchez against the defending champion, Stanton. The Miami fans were cheering loudly for their hometown hero. Sanchez got hot and whacked 17 out of the park to open the round. Now Stanton had four minutes to pass him. He came close but only hit 16. With Stanton out of the contest most eyes focused on Aaron Judge. After Cody Bellinger eliminated Charlie Blackmon, 16–14, it was time for Aaron to go up against another home-town favorite, Justin Bour.

Suddenly the lefty-swinging Bour was whacking one home run after another and the Miami fans went wild. He even took a timeout to let Stanton put a doughnut into his mouth. Then he stepped back into the box and hit seven home runs in seven swings. He had smacked 22 home runs, a daunting total for anyone to pass, even Aaron Judge.

But after a little bit of a slow start, Aaron began hitting moonshots. Slowly the gap closed as even the Miami fans had to cheer what they were watching. Aaron kept swinging and the balls continued to fly out of the park. On one swing, Aaron hit the ball so high that it hit the closed roof of Marlin's stadium. According to the ground rules, it didn't count. At the end of four minutes he had 21 home runs, but he had earned the extra time because of the length of his home runs. That's when he slammed two more and won the round, 23–22.

After that, it was almost a foregone conclusion as to the outcome. Aaron then took out fellow rookie Cody Bellinger, 13–12, a round in which he hit three, 500-foot home runs, including two in a row of 504 and 513 feet. In the finals, he followed Miguel Sano, who hit 10 home runs. Aaron then stepped up and hit 11 homers in just 15 swings to win the competition. There was still 1:53 left on the clock. In this season of seasons, Aaron Judge had now won the Home Run Derby.

"It was a blast," Aaron said, afterward. "I enjoyed every minute of it—watching the other guys swing, coming here early and talking to the media. Everything about today was fantastic. It was just an incredible experience. There was a lot of the unknown and I think that's kind of what motivated me, to see how good you can be."

Many of the other players were in awe of Aaron's performance. Former Yankee and derby winner Robinson Cano said, "What he did was amazing. I've never seen anything like that. Not only the home runs, but to go opposite field that many times. He made this ballpark look like nothing. I've seen it all before, but this guy, he's on another level. He doesn't even look tired."

Mookie Betts, who played for the rival Red Sox, also couldn't say enough about Aaron.

"When you walk up to him, he's way bigger than you think he is. He looks like he belongs in the NBA. Obviously, his ability's gotten him to where he is, but that's not the amazing part. It's just that he's so big. For a human to get like that is pretty amazing to me."

Aaron was the talk of the town after his performance in the Home Run Derby. Since the event was nationally televised, more people saw not only his huge home runs, but his humble yet engaging personality, characterized by a perpetual smile and genuine feeling of joy just being there. He never took his talent for granted, worked hard to improve and refine it, and considered everything that had happened to him a blessing.

ALL RISE

The game itself was anticlimactic. The American League won, 2–1, in ten innings. But the game no longer determined home field advantage in the World Series. That practice had been abandoned. Now the team with the best record would earn home field. Aaron was hitless in three at-bats during the game, but none of that really mattered. Fans in Miami and those who watched on television were still talking about his incredible performance the night before. The big man had truly made an impression.

THE SLUMP BEGINS

There has always been some concern about players participating in the Home Run Derby. Some feel that by consciously trying to hit home runs a player might alter his swing and that could affect him when the regular season resumes. Some players have gone into slumps after the derby. Others have had a home run drought. But Aaron had been swinging like that all season long to the tune of 30 home runs and a .300 plus batting average. He had struck out quite often, but that was to be expected from such a big guy with a long swing. Strikeouts, in fact, were up all over the league, as were home runs. So the prevailing thought was that Aaron would take up just about where he left off.

It didn't happen. While the Yankees played very solid ball the rest of July, winning 12 of 18 games with a six-game winning streak thrown in, Aaron came out of the break and immediately began struggling. He had just one hit in his first 15 at-bats starting with the resumption of play on July 14, and that was a dribbler in front of the plate. Before the month was out he did hit four more homers, but he was also striking out more and seemingly missing pitches he had hit earlier in the year.

With rookies it's often said the second and third time around the league is the toughest. Once the pitchers begin to find a weakness they'll exploit it and the word spreads quickly. Then it's up to the hitter to adjust. When Aaron reached the majors he adjusted by abandoning a high leg kick he'd used in the minors and stood slightly farther off the plate. He also worked on using the lower half of his body better with each swing.

"The big thing is learning which off-speed pitches to swing at," Aaron had said. "A lot of people say, 'Oh, this guy can't hit a curveball; this guy can't hit an off-speed pitch.' But it's about swinging at the right one. Swing at the hangers. Swing at the ones you can handle."

Before the season, pitchers felt they could get him out with breaking balls, but he was proving them wrong. Now, suddenly, he was swinging and missing at the low, outside breaking ball. At the same time, fastballs up and in were often tying him up. By the beginning of August, it was apparent he was dealing with his first slump of the season. Slumps happen to the best of them at one time or another and each hitter has to figure the best way to break them. The question was how Aaron would deal with it.

By August 2, the slump was undeniable. Aaron's batting average had dropped 30 points in the two weeks since the All-Star break ended, dipping under .300 for the first time all year. He had been batting either in the two or three spot in the lineup since he got hot early in the season. Manager Girardi said he had no plans to move him down. But he was also striking out in nearly half his at-bats since the All-Star break. Shades of last season.

"I'm just missing my pitches," Aaron said. "When you get it, you just can't miss." Then he added, "We all have to make adjustments."

That was because the team as a whole wasn't hitting well. Matt Holliday, who had been so good the first few months before the viral infection felled him, was still struggling, as were others. With the team still feeling it could make the playoffs, GM Cashman had made several deals at the July 31, trade deadline, giving up a number of the team's fine prospects. From the White Sox the Yanks received relief pitchers David Robertson and Tommy Kahnle, as well as third baseman Todd Frazier. And in another trade, with Oakland, the Yanks acquired right-handed pitcher Sonny Gray, considered one of the top pitchers in the league.

Would the roster tweak work? Robertson had been with the Yankees earlier in his career and was a proven commodity. He could close or take on a setup role. Kahnle had also once been in the Yankee organization and had emerged as another late-inning power arm. Todd Frazier was an outstanding third sacker who had good power, though didn't hit for average. His presence would push Chase Headley from third to first, where the Yanks still hadn't found a suitable replacement for Greg Bird. But the biggest thing troubling the team continued to be Aaron's Judge's batting slump, which was showing no signs of abating.

As the Yankees headed to Cleveland to begin a road trip in early August, Aaron had hit just .164 in the previous 19 games, going 11-for-67 with just nine RBIs. Manager Girardi tried to make it simple.

"I don't think pitchers are really pitching him a whole lot different," he said. "I think that he's been off a little bit mechanically, and some of the balls he was hitting before, he's missing. I don't think he's staying on the ball long enough. These are things that we need to get him to do."

The old tried-and-true eye test saw Aaron missing fastballs up and in, as well as breaking balls low and away. Despite his long arms, he was swinging at some pitches that were impossible to reach. And there were even times when he'd whiff on fastballs over the heart of the plate. These are all earmarks of an old-fashioned slump. Finally, on August 3, Manager Girardi gave Aaron a day off against the Indians and their ace pitcher, Corey Kluber.

"It's just he's struggling, and we felt we'd give him a day off and maybe it helps him," Girardi said. "You try to do it a lot of different ways when guys are struggling, and I just felt maybe a day off would do him some good."

Aaron did hit a homer on August 6, but it didn't lead to a hot streak. Things got worse for the team two days later when CC Sabathia hurt his knee and had to go on the disabled list. It was yet another injury and the Yankees were simply looking like a .500 ballclub—win one, lose one—and now trailing first-place Boston by four games.

By August 10, it was still apparent that Aaron had not come out of the slump. In his past 84 at-bats he had 14 hits, was batting .167 with five home runs and 38 strikeouts. That was compared with his 2016 call-up when he had 15 hits in 84 at-bats, a .179 batting average, four homers, and 44 strikeouts. The numbers were eerily similar, which begged the question: Who was the real Aaron Judge? Was it the guy who electrified the baseball world in the first half of the season, or the guy who struck out in half his at-bats and hit an occasional monster home run? Or maybe the answer was somewhere in between.

There were other problems for the team as well. Gary Sanchez was hitting for power and driving in runs, but on defense was having problems blocking pitches, a necessity for today's catchers with pitchers throwing sliders and split-fingered fastballs that often dip into the dirt. Aaron Hicks had a second oblique injury, and then Clint Frazier suffered the same injury. Young Luis Severino had emerged as the ace of the staff, but star pitcher Masahiro Tanaka had been inconsistent. Now Sabathia, having a bounceback season was on the DL. Newcomer Sonny Gray was pitching well, but not getting a lot of run support. Even closer Aroldis Chapman had lost his edge for a couple of weeks.

On August 12, the Yanks were blown out by Boston, 10–5, to fall four-and-a-half games behind. They also got the news that pitcher Tanaka had to go on the DL with arm soreness. Things were going from bad to worse and Aaron wasn't helping. Since the All-Star break, Aaron had struck out 43 times and, amazingly, had fanned at least once in 29 straight games. His batting average was down to .289 from .329 at the break. He still had a fine .419 on-base percentage due to him still drawing walks.

To Aaron's credit, his demeanor never changed. He answered questions with his usual smile, preferred to talk about the team, but didn't deflect questions about his slump. He acknowledged he was struggling, but he also remained optimistic and felt he would come out of it.

"I'm still holding up great," he said. "For me, it's just that time of year. Everyone goes through these ups and downs. You are going to get out of this. It's just part of baseball. Those 0-for-4 days make those 4-for-4 days so much better. I just have to keep grinding; it will all work out. The pitches I'm fouling off now

I would usually be putting in play. I just have to keep grinding."

There was no sign of Aaron getting down on himself or frustrated. He seemed to honestly feel that this kind of slump, no matter how difficult and unpleasant, was part of the game and he would come out of it. The slump had also not affected his popularity. The fans still flocked to see him, cheered wildly for him, and at Yankee Stadium the Judge's Chambers were always filled and vibrant.

It was also announced in mid-August that Aaron had signed an endorsement deal with Fanatics, a company that is one of the leaders in officially licensed sports merchandise and one that had under contract other young stars such as Kris Bryant and Anthony Rizzo of the Cubs, as well as Corey Seager and Cody Bellinger of the Dodgers. Players today can make big bucks with commercial endorsements but Aaron, despite many offers, was being careful.

"I've been pretty selective with who I want to partner with," he explained. "For me, Fanatics seemed like the right fit. Now fans, not only in the New York area, but around the world can get my products and my autographs. I'm excited to do that."

Aaron said the new deal would not stop him from signing autographs for fans at the various ballparks. "I love signing for fans, especially Yankee fans," he said. "They are the best in the world. Fanatics also has some pretty cool pictures of me. I'm not going to lie: I'm looking forward to getting those out."

But priority number one was to help the Yankees get back to winning ways. Aaron homered on August 14 and again two days later. Maybe he was breaking out it. They would be, however, the last home runs he'd hit in August, giving him a total of three for the month, not something a top slugger looks to do.

Aaron's home run on August 16, was a 536-foot blast at Citi Field that helped the Yankees to a 5–3 victory over the crosstown Mets. It was his 37th of the season, still good enough to lead the American League but only his seventh since the All-Star break. He also struck out in his final at-bat of the game, giving him a record he probably didn't want. It marked the 33rd straight game that he had fanned, longest mark ever by a non-pitcher in a single season. His 159 strikeouts were second-most in the majors to another slugger, Miguel Sano of Minnesota.

"There are great pitchers in this league," he said. "You're going to get fooled sometimes; they're going to get you. If I keep taking my right swings and swing at the right pitches, good things will happen. People strike out. I strike out a lot—it happens. Just got to keep working.

"If I feel good, I'm happy with that. The results will come or won't come. It's just about sticking with the process, sticking with what I know is going to work. If I do that, good things usually happen. [A slump] is one of the hardest things in the game, because you always want to have success. But you've got to still believe in the process, believe in everything. Everybody goes through ups and downs."

Those were the words of an optimist. It was apparent Aaron still believed in himself, still felt he was going to come out of a slump that was now going into its second month. The Yankees and everyone else just hoped it would be soon.

With all the questions thrown at Aaron during his rookie season, people were gradually learning more and more about Aaron Judge the man. A reporter asked him about what so many have noticed, why he never watches his home run, just puts his head down and runs. Aaron readily explained why:

In my senior year in high school, I had a ton of major-league scouts at the game. I thought it would be cool to kind of show off. In my first at-bat I hit a ball to center field that I thought was a long way out. So I started watching. And then I started to take a nice little jog to first. The ball hit right off the top of the wall and I didn't even make it to second base. After that happened I said that would be the last time I don't hustle.

Lesson learned and nothing's changed. No posing, no bat-flipping, none of the so-called flair that so many in the game practice now. When a guy Aaron's size hits one 450–500 feet, that's what the fans want to see. They don't care whether he poses, pounds his chest, makes gestures to his teammates, all the things you see today. Aaron's philosophy was old-school. You hit the ball and you run.

Only now, he wanted to hit it more often. He continued to hit third in the lineup though many people felt Manager Girardi should move him down. The manager disagreed.

"He's going to stay there," Girardi said "I'm not going to move him. He's still dangerous. He's still getting on [base] at a pretty high clip. He's on in front of some other guys who are swinging the bat well."

But by Monday, August 21, someone pointed out that Aaron was hitting just .170 since the All-Star break and the day before had extended his major-league record by striking out at least once in 37 straight games. He also had just one hit in his last 16 at-bats and wasn't making hard contact. It was growing into a slump of epic proportions and maybe on the brink of ruining one of the feel-good seasons of the ages. But then another factor became part of the equation.

After that Sunday, August 20, game with the Red Sox in which Aaron was 0–4 and saw his season's average drop to .282, he came out to face reporters with his left shoulder wrapped in ice, something pitchers often do to reduce swelling after throwing many pitches. This had apparently been part of his postgame routine for a while and something he rarely spoke about. He would just say it was nothing serious and had nothing to do with his slump. He just wasn't one to make excuses.

Any small injury, any kind of ache or pain that would alter a hitter's swing in just the slightest way, could throw him off just enough to cause a slump. Even a bruise to the front shoulder could cause a problem. But Aaron hadn't missed any games and said he didn't intend to take a seat. Some speculated that maybe a stint on the DL would help, but the Yankees apparently didn't feel it was necessary. He continued to play.

Instead of dropping Aaron in the lineup, Manager Joe Girardi flip-flopped him with a hot Gary Sanchez. Aaron moved up to the second spot; Sanchez down to the third. Sanchez belted a pair of homers in a 13–4 win over the Tigers on August 22, while Aaron reached base four times on an RBI single and three walks, and also ended his strikeout string at 37 games. Sanchez had 11 homers in his last 24 games, with one of his blasts against the Tigers going 493 feet. The only person to hit one farther was Aaron, whose best was 495 feet.

"I think I've still got him by two feet," Aaron quipped, joking with Sanchez. "That was pretty impressive, but I can brag."

The Yanks were still four-and-a-half games behind Boston and entering a stretch run that would see them play 39 games in 41 days. And everyone was still trying to pinpoint why Aaron still hadn't broken his slump. Tom Wilson, who was Aaron's hitting coach at Scranton the season before, felt it was a mechanical problem. He felt part of it was head movement, which he said changes the "read mode." He equated his problems with that of the Yanks six-foot-eight reliever, Dellin Betances.

"As big a person as [Judge] is, well, it's like Dellin," said Wilson. "When his mechanics are a click off, he's all over the place. They have a similar body type. Now Judge's mechanics and timing are a little off and for him. It looks catastrophic. And it is."

Then on August 26, came *the brawl*. As is often the case in baseball, it was caused by beanballs, players getting hit by pitches. The Yankees were playing the Tigers in Detroit. There was some bad blood between the two teams from earlier in the season. It began that day when the Tigers Michael Fullmer hit Jacoby Ellsbury in the hip. Then Sanchez was plunked by Fullmer after hitting a homer earlier in the game. When Yankee reliever Tommy Kahnle threw a pitch behind Miguel Cabrera with two outs in the sixth, Kahnle and Joe Girardi were ejected.

After Cabrera got back in the batter's box, he exchanged words with Yankee catcher Austin Romine. Cabrera pushed Romine, then threw a punch. Romine then tackled Carbrera and the benches quickly emptied. Several players were on the ground when it appeared Sanchez threw a punch at one of the Tigers. Romine and Cabrera were then ejected, but it wasn't over yet. In the seventh, the Tigers' James McCann was hit in the head by Dellin Betances as he led off the inning. Once again, the benches emptied and this time Betances and bench coach Rob Thomson were ejected. In the eighth, the Tigers Alex Wilson hit Todd Frazier, causing the benches to empty for a third time. Wilson was bounced from the game. To make it worse, the Yankees lost the game, 10–6.

It didn't help when Sanchez later got a four-game suspension for his role. Others received lesser suspensions, but it was just another setback in a season that was still on the brink. Cabrera even claimed that Aaron threw a punch at his throat during the pushing and shoving that goes on in baseball brawls. He felt Aaron should be suspended also. Cabrera (who originally got a seven-game ban, later reduced to six, as Sanchez's suspension was reduced from five to four games) was the one accusing Aaron.

When Aaron heard that he simply shrugged it off. "That's old news," he said. [MLB] looked at the video."

The only positive thing that can come out of an ugly incident such as this is that it can bring a team together as players stand up for each other. Right about now, the Yankees could use it. They were basically playing .500 ball for the month of August, and if they continued to falter, they could miss the play-offs entirely. They still held one of the two wild-card spots but wanted to win the division. To do that, they and Aaron would both have to pick up the pace. They would also need some help from Greg Bird, who was called up after a rehab stint at Scranton following his surgery. His ankle finally seemed healed and he quickly took over the first-base job.

Toward the end of the month, Girardi decided to give Aaron a couple of days off. Nothing else seemed to help. He hadn't hit a homer in almost two weeks and was still struggling at the plate. For the first time, Aaron admitted his body was beat up from the long season. He talked about the possibility of getting a cortisone shot in his left shoulder, acknowledging that the shoulder he was icing was something of a problem.

"I've got ice on my shoulders, my knees. I wish I could ice my whole body," Aaron said. "I've got to ice every day. The whole body is kind of beat up. I think it's just the grind of the season. It's kind of the body wearing down. You've got to make adjustments and fight through that."

He was still hitting just .179 since the All-Star break with just seven home runs and 16 RBIs. As August drew to a close, everyone wondered how Aaron would fare in September. Manager Girardi even said he was considering more rest for his big slugger. Much would depend how September began. Aaron still felt he was going to bounce back.

"Like I've said all year, if I'm swinging at the right pitches, taking my walks, I feel like I'm in a good place to hit," he said. "I have to build off one day and then take it into the next."

He didn't consider the two days off a mental break from the game. But he said it was strange, just sitting around without even swinging a bat.

"I haven't done that all year," he said. "I've been going stir-crazy. My routine has been messed up. So it's been kind of weird for me." Then he added, "Refresh the body, that's been the biggest thing. Get a little refresher here for the last push. We've got some important games coming up."

CHAPTER SIX

A REVIVAL, AND JUST IN TIME

🏆

IN A 9–4 LOSS TO Cleveland on August 30, the return-ing Greg Bird hit a three-run homer and drove in all four runs for the Yankees. A rejuvenated and healthy Bird would be a big boost to the offense. But having Aaron Judge perform the way he did the first half of the season would be an even bigger boost. When the team began their September push with a 4–1 loss to the Red Sox, their season record was just 71–63 and they trailed the Sox by five-and-a-half games in the divisional race. There were now just 28 games left.

For that game with the Red Sox, Manager Girardi moved Aaron down to the number-six spot in the lineup, a move many had been suggesting since his long slump began. As with all that had happened to him during the season, the highs and the lows, Aaron took this move in stride. He continued to stay positive and level-headed. There was never a sign of him getting down on himself or even pouting.

"I'm just a player," he said. "It doesn't matter where they put me. I'm just excited to be in the lineup."

Aaron also said his left shoulder "feels good," and that getting a couple of days off earlier in the week had really seemed to help him out.

"I've been going every day since April 2, or whatever," he said. "So getting a couple of days off, I think, helped it for the long haul."

But the long haul was now getting short. Veteran Matt Holliday was the latest to predict that Aaron was ready to break out. He had been close with Aaron since the beginning of the season, serving as a friend and mentor.

"It looks like the timing is going to be awesome," Holliday said. "When you come out of these things, especially when you have the talent [Aaron] has, it comes out big. He carried us for a long time in the first half. There's a stretch of that coming, and it's gonna be good timing. I'm excited about what's coming."

Holliday made that statement on September 2, the same day Masahiro Tanaka beat the Red Sox, 5–1. The next day, Aaron brought the crowd to its feet with a 469-foot home run in a 9–2 Yankee victory. It was his first home run since August 16, and it snapped a season-long run of 57 at-bats without a homer. It was also his 38th of the year. Was it the beginning of Holliday's prophecy or just a tease?

Holliday, for one, felt it was going to continue.

"When you're that big and strong and talented, eventually you're gonna start hitting home runs again."

On September 7, Aaron hit another in a big Yankees 9–1 win over Baltimore behind the pitching of Sonny Gray. The team had won four of six games since the new month began and now it was looking as if the big guy was tuning up again. After the game, Aaron was asked about his season, whether he was satisfied where he was going into the final month of the season. He said:

"[My numbers] are not where I want them to be. There are a lot of missed opportunities throughout the year, if you want me to look back at it right now. But I just have to keep working. I'm not really satisfied because you can always get better. We've got a good opportunity as a team to do something special this year, so I have to keep going to work."

He sounded more like a veteran than a rookie and once again focused on the team. And right away he focused on the playoffs.

"That's what it's all about," he said. "That's what I dreamed about as a kid. Not just making the play-offs, but making it to the World Series and winning a World Series. That's our goal, to win our division and make a run in these playoffs. It means everything."

The Yankees were still leading in the wild-card race. But since there are two wild-card teams, and a single game between them to see which team advances, the team certainly preferred to win the division and not have to play a one-and-done game. After their win on September 7, they trailed the first-place Red Sox by three-and-a-half games. So it was still possible for them to take the division.

Though Aaron was far from done, Manager Girardi pointed out something else about his season.

"I think he's had a really good year," the manager said. "When you look at his numbers, he's walked 100 times, he's scored 100 runs, and there's a really good chance that he's going to get 100 RBIs."

It was also pointed out that Aaron had become the first rookie in 64 years to walk 100 times. This showed that despite his slump, pitchers still feared him and worked him carefully. Although he was leading the league in strikeouts, he was also walking more than anyone. That kept his on-base percentage high. While his accomplishments to date were impressive, even with the slump, no one was prepared for what was to come in the final weeks.

In a September 10 game against Texas, the Yankees offense really unloaded. The Bombers won the game 16–7, as Aaron and Gary Sanchez hit two home runs apiece. For Sanchez, who missed the first month of the season with an injury, they were home run numbers 29 and 30. And for Aaron, it was yet another milestone. He blasted numbers 40 and 41, putting him in very elite company. He was now just the second rookie in major-league history to hit 40 or more home runs. Mark McGwire held the rookie record of 49, set back in 1989.

Only four other Yankees in the team's storied history had hit 40 or more home runs in their age-25 season, and those names were perhaps the most iconic in franchise annals. Babe Ruth, Lou Gehrig, Joe DiMaggio, and Mickey Mantle. Now Aaron Judge had put his name alongside theirs.

"Pretty surreal," Aaron said, when informed of the select company he had joined. "Never as a kid would I ever think that I'd be in the same sentence as those guys. It's quite an honor. It's pretty humbling."

Aaron also drew a walk in the game, his 107th free pass of the season, and that set yet another major-league record. He had now walked more times than any other rookie in history. Even during his slump, he continued to draw walks and he said that was part of his overall game.

"Just getting on base," he said. "With the team I have around me, all I have to do is get on base for them and they'll drive me in. My goal all year has been to get on base with a knock or a walk."

In the past seven games, Aaron had hit .292 with four home runs. It was beginning to look like the breakout so many had predicted for him, but, in reality, he was just getting started. And better yet, the Yankees had won seven of their last 10 games as they continued to chase the Red Sox. Aaron was definitely looking better at the plate and, four days later, he proved it by going yard again. Twice.

In a 13–5 victory over Baltimore on September 14, Aaron hit a pair of three-run homers for a career best six runs batted in. His now led the league with 43 home runs and had 96 RBIs for the season. Gary Sanchez followed Aaron's second homer with a shot of his own, his 31st of the season. The two young players were becoming a formidable duo of power hitters, both developed in the Yankee farm system and promising to wield their lethal bats for years to come. Aaron, always the great teammate, preferred to talk about Sanchez rather than himself.

"I'm excited to see what Gary can do in a full season," he said. "He missed a month and still put up those kinds of numbers."

The team had now won five of six games to pull within three of Boston. With Aaron Judge suddenly hitting home runs in bunches once again, the big offense of the first half had returned as many echoed the sentiment, "As goes Judge, so go the Yankees." A hot Aaron Judge was definitely a game-changer. It was obvious in the first half of the season when he was the most exciting player in baseball, and it was resurfacing now at the most important part of the season.

Now that Aaron was heating up again, there was renewed talk about the Most Valuable Player award, given after the season. It was almost a foregone conclusion that he would be the Rookie of the Year choice. The last player to win both in the same year was Seattle's Ichiro Suzuki in 2001 and the only other player to do it before him was the Red Sox' Fred Lynn in 1975. During the first half of the season it was pretty much acknowledged that Aaron was the league's Most Valuable Player. The long slump brought him back to the pack. But his apparent resurgence in September once again put him in the race. His chief competition was thought to be Houston's little second sacker, Jose Altuve, who was in the midst of a great season. But awards weren't on Aaron's mind. Winning and getting into the playoffs were. That's what counted the most.

On September 18, the Yanks defeated the Minnesota Twins, 2–1, taking the lead early on Aaron's first-inning homer, his 44th of the season. Todd Frazier drove in the winning run with a sacrifice fly in the sixth, and

Aroldis Chapman closed it out in fine fashion. The only blip on the radar was reliever Dellin Betances, who was having command problems again. When right, Betances was one of the most dominant relievers in the league. Like Aaron, he was a huge man at six-foot-eight, and if his mechanics (his pitching motion) were slightly off, he'd lose the plate. Chapman had his own struggles early, but once again looked like the dominant closer he always had been.

The team was also getting great bullpen work from young Chad Green, as well as veterans David Robertson and Tommy Kahnle, the two pitchers the Yanks acquired at the trade deadline. The returning Robertson had closed for them when Mariano Rivera retired. He then went to the White Sox. He said it felt like he was "home" again and was pitching great. Except for Betances' slump, the bullpen was doing a great job, especially during the September run.

With Greg Bird back and contributing, he and short-stop Gregorius gave the Yankees two left-handed power bats to complement Aaron and Gary Sanchez from the right side. In addition, Aaron's 44th home run put him within five of Mark McGwire's longstanding rookie record. During his slump, most felt he wouldn't reach the record, but his recent surge renewed interest in his chase of McGwire's mark, though that was something else he just wouldn't talk about.

"It'd be pretty surreal," he said, using one of his favorite words, "but that's the last thing on my mind right now, to be honest, especially with what we got going on here in the last couple of games. We're fighting to win a division. Home-run races, they come second to that."

But there was one home-run story that did make all the papers and sports shows. When Alex Gordon of the Royals hit a home run against the Toronto Blue Jays on September 18, it was the 5,694th home run of the 2017 season, a new major-league record, topping the old record of set in 2000, which was at the height of the so-called Steroid Era. Home runs had subsided after drug testing increased and in 2014 only 4,186 dingers were hit.

Since then, the game had changed somewhat. More players were trying to hit the ball out, swinging from their heels as opposed to just trying to put the ball in play. Some of the newer ballparks were smaller. Some people also said the ball was "juiced" in 2017, that it was made to travel farther than the previous baseballs. Major League Baseball denied this, but many of the players felt that it was true, and some independent tests also indicated the ball was slightly different. Home runs, especially long homers, had always been something fans love, going back to the days of Babe Ruth.

That's one reason Aaron Judge had become such a sensation. His home runs were often majestic, high and deep, and traveled farther and faster than anyone else's. It was also said that when he hit the ball just right, the sound of the bat hitting the ball was different from others. In the National League, Giancarlo Stanton, another big slugger, had hit even more than Aaron and said he wanted to reach 60. That kept the home run in the news in both leagues with Aaron's September resurgence again putting him on top of the sports pages.

As well as Aaron had performed in September, there was more to come as he was about to get hotter than hot. On September 20, he whacked number 45 as the Yanks topped Minnesota, 11–3. His solo shot and a subsequent sacrifice fly gave him 101 RBIs on the season. He joined Joe DiMaggio, Tony Lazzeri, and Hideki Matsui as the only Yankees to reach the 100-RBI mark as rookies.

Two days later he slammed number 46 for the Yankees only run as they lost to Toronto, 8–1. He was no longer icing his shoulder after games and while he never used it as an excuse, many now felt that it was a sore shoulder that contributed to his post All-Star Game slump. He also showed his level-headedness and a veteran approach to the game when he spoke about playing in the huge New York market: "One thing I've realized is that there's a lot of noise that comes with playing here. It's not a bad thing; it comes with the territory. But it's important not to listen to that noise. If I do, then an 0-for-4 will automatically turn into an 0-for-8 or worse. I have to remind myself that the 0-for-4s are part of baseball and it's a long season. You're going to have ups and downs."

Rookie outfielder Clint Frazier, who played well after his mid-season call-up until an oblique injury put him on the shelf, marveled at the way fellow rookie Judge was able to handle the avalanche of attention he was getting and still remain calm.

"There's no way I could have handled all the attention Aaron got, at the beginning and then [after the All-Star break]. He's just a really easygoing guy."

But the easygoing guy was once again a terror with the bat. On September 24, he slammed a pair of four-baggers even though the team lost to Toronto, 9–5. That gave him 48 on the season, just one behind

McGwire's rookie record. At the beginning of the month very few gave him a chance to even approach the mark. The only problem was that the Red Sox were also winning and the Yankees still trailed their rivals by five full games. The day before, however, they had clinched a wild-card berth with a 5–1 win over the Blue Jays. But Judge and his teammates didn't quit. They still wanted to try to win the division.

The resurgent Greg Bird said, "The middle of the lineup, they've been producing all year, and when they go, we go. This lineup is great, and it's just fun to be a part of right now."

It was also pointed out that Aaron was again taking the ball to right field and hitting home runs the other way, as he had done in the first half. As Manager Girardi said, "You can talk about the home runs and the RBIs, but it's the on-base percentage and the base running and the defense, too. It's the complete package that we've gotten from him. That's what's been so impressive to me."

The complete package had also joined another very exclusive club, joining Hall of Famer Ted Williams as the only rookies in major-league history to reach the 100 mark in RBIs, runs scored, and walks in their first seasons. It seemed as if his season was becoming more incredible every day. And he wasn't through yet.

One day after hitting a pair of homers against Toronto at the Rogers Center, Aaron and the Yanks returned home to face the Kansas City Royals. The big crowd at the Stadium knew that another home run would tie Mark McGwire's rookie record. Everyone was on the edge of the seats every time Aaron came to bat, and he didn't disappoint. He not only tied the record with his 49th home run, he surpassed it when he belted his 50th and second of the game. It was the icing on the cake, his second straight two-home-run game and a new rookie record.

Being the first rookie to hit 50 home runs in a season once again put Aaron on the top of the sports world and the accolades rolled in. There were more calls for him to win the MVP in addition to Rookie of the Year, which was already a lock. The amazing thing with all the current hoopla, and what had come before, is that Aaron hadn't changed a bit since opening day. Even after he hit his 50th and the Stadium crowd called for him to come out of the dugout for a curtain call, it was his teammates who urged him to step out. He did, but Aaron admitted he was embarrassed by it all.

"The game was still going on," Aaron said. He didn't want to be a distraction.

After it was over, veteran Todd Frazier, who had joined the team at the trade deadline, explained why he and his teammates admired Aaron so much.

"He went through [his long slump] and just kept working," Frazier said. "That's very hard to come back from, but that's his mentality, his personality. It's incredible, hitting 50 home runs and for him to be as humble as he is. It's an honor to play with him."

Manager Girardi, who had seen many come and go as a player, a coach, and then a manager, called Aaron "a natural born leader. He's like a big brother who watches over everybody. You've got the whole package with him."

Another veteran Yankee, Chase Headley, admired the way Aaron went about his business on the field. "It's fun to watch someone hit a long, long home run and just put his head down and go, and not show anybody up. Let the swing speak for itself. It's refreshing. The swing is just different. It's like a seven-foot basketball player on a nine-foot goal."

The only thing Aaron did as he crossed the plate after hitting number 50 was point skyward. Later he explained, "The Lord put me in this position. I took a quick moment to say thank you. It's a blessing every time I step on that field."

After the game, stadium personnel were able to get both the 49th and 50th home-run baseballs back for Aaron. When Judge was asked what he planned to do with them, his answer was easy.

"I'll probably give them to my parents," he said. "Especially for all the sacrifices they've made for me throughout the years, those 25 years. It means the world to me to get them [back]."

It was pointed out that Aaron now had 13 home runs in just 75 at-bats in September. While he led the Yankees to a 38–23 record at the start of the season with his sensational play, his resurgence had helped the team to a 16–6 mark in September. The fact that Aaron had come out of a long slump to once again be the dynamic star he was in the first half of the season certainly augured well for the Yankees. But there were still games to be played.

Oh, yes, there was still another big fan of Aaron's. Mark McGwire, whose record Aaron had broken, had gone from admitted user of performance-enhancing drugs to a respected batting coach. He was very impressed by what he saw of Aaron Judge.

"I'm a fan," big Mac said. "I'm a fan of his game. I was watching from day one. I mean, they're monstrous home runs. His BPs (batting practices) are going to be legendary. He's only 25 years old. Who knows what the number is going to be by the time he's done. Even though he's struck out, what, 200 times this year, I consider him a very patient hitter because he's walking over 100 times. He's going to hit .300 someday and drive in 100 runs every year."

It was hard to remember another player of recent vintage who had caused the excitement and interest, the accolades and speculation, that Aaron Judge has caused. It sometimes seemed his name was on the mind of every baseball fan, writer, sports talk host, and even his fellow players for the entire season. His September revival brought back all the good feelings of the first half that culminated in his epic Home Run Derby victory. With the Yankees most likely going to the playoffs via the wild-card route, he and his teammates were focused on advancing as far as they could. And as far that meant making it to the World Series.

But Aaron's regular season wasn't quite over yet. On September 28, he whacked his 51st home run and two days later slammed his 52nd against Toronto. That shot, off the Jays' Marcus Stroman, traveled 484 feet, his second-longest homer of the season. It was almost a final reminder of what he could do. He also set a new Yankees record by hitting 33 of his home runs at the Stadium. The former record-holder: Babe Ruth. The Babe had hit 32 at home way back in 1921 when the Yankees shared the Polo Grounds with the New York Giants.

The Yanks closed the regular season the next day, on October 1, dropping their final game, 2–1, to the Blue Jays. But the team's 20–8 record in September brought their season mark to 91–71, and they finished two games behind division-winning Boston. That left them to play the do-or-die wild-card game against the Minnesota Twins at Yankee Stadium. The team had exceeded all preseason expectations, and so had Aaron Judge.

Aaron simply had an incredible rookie season. In addition to his rookie record and league-leading 52 home runs, he also led the league with 127 walks and 128 runs scored. He was second in the league with 114 runs batted in and hit a solid .284. He had 24 doubles, three triples, and even stole nine bases in 13 tries.

Not bad for a man of his size. The only negative stat was that he also led the league with 208 strikeouts. Many came during the slump, but a big man with a big swing will always have his share of strikeouts. With his other numbers, any team would put up with that. And with Aaron's history of making adjustments, it won't be surprising to see his strikeout numbers come down in future years.

In September alone, Aaron hit .311, with 15 home runs and 32 runs batted in to really put a stamp on his season. When the great Babe Ruth hit his then record 60 home runs in 1927, he exploded for the final 17 in September. Aaron came close to duplicating that, hitting his final 15 when they counted the most, when the team was fighting for the postseason.

You can make a case for Aaron being the prime mover in the Yankees surprising season, but baseball is obviously a team game and the big guy had plenty of help. Catcher Sanchez provided a second big bat in the lineup, hitting .278 with 33 home runs and 90 runs batted in. Shortstop Didi Gregorius continued to improve and was becoming another star player. He hit .287 with career bests 27 home runs and 87 RBIs. He, like Sanchez, missed a full month at the beginning of the season.

Second sacker Starlin Castro hit an even .300 with 16 homers and 63 ribbies in just 112 games (due to hamstring injuries), while veteran left fielder Brett Gardner continued to be a sparkplug with a .264 average, 21 home runs, 63 RBIs, and 23 stolen bases. The team also got strong contributions from Aaron Hicks, Todd Frazier, Chase Headley, and even utility infielder Ronald Torreyes. The returning Greg Bird hit just .190, due in part to hitting only .100 early in the season with his ankle injury. But he hit eight of his nine homers after his late-season return and once again showed his great potential as a lefty-swinging power hitter.

Young right-hander Luis Severino became the ace of the staff, finishing with a 14–6 record and 2.98 earned run average to go along with 230 strikeouts. He would become one of the three finalists for the Cy Young Award, given to the best pitcher in the league. Masahiro Tanaka had a strong finish to an up-and-down season, winding up with a 13–12 record, while 37-year-old CC Sabathia surprised everyone by compiling a 14–5 record with a solid 3.69 ERA. Even rookie left-hander Jordan Montgomery contributed with a 9–7 mark.

The bullpen was extremely solid, led by closer Chapman, vets David Robertson and Adam Warren, as well as youngsters Tommy Kahnle and Chad Green. Only Dellin Betances took a step back with some very erratic performances. All in all, this surprising Yankee team exceeded expectations on many levels. But there was still more business at hand as the playoffs lay ahead.

CHAPTER SEVEN

ON TO THE POSTSEASON

🏆

THE WAY BASEBALL IS SET up now, becoming one of the two wild-card teams in each league doesn't mean too much. In theory, a team is in the playoffs, but the wild–card game is essentially sudden death. The winning team moves on to the best of five division series, while the loser goes home. That's why it would have been much better to win the division outright. Since the Yankees had the best record of the two wild-card teams (the Twins being the other), the game would be played at Yankee Stadium.

As for Aaron, he could hardly contain his excitement about going to the postseason his rookie year. He felt the team just had to keep up their strong September play to make a run.

"Just keep playing our game," he said. "Keep doing what we've been doing the past couple of weeks and keep having fun. [I] never played for a team like this, where everyone gets along. We're always competing, we're always having fun. That's what championship teams are made of, so I'm excited for what's gonna happen in the postseason."

The American League wild-card game was held at the Stadium on October 4, with the Yanks' Luis Severino opposing the Twins best pitcher, Ervin Santana. The Yankees were favorites, especially with Severino pitching. Aaron felt the tension of the one-game format and admitted he was nervous before the game, right through batting practice and the introduction of the players.

"Yes, I was nervous before the game, but after the first pitch was thrown I was fine. I realized it's still the same game we've been playing since we were kids."

But after just a few minutes, he and his teammates, as well as the more than 49,000 fans at Yankee Stadium, were more than a little bit worried. For one of the few times this season, Severino didn't have it. Brian Dozier led off for the Twins in the first inning and promptly hit a home run into the left-field seats. Three batters later, with one out and one on, Eddie Rosario hit one out to give the Twins a three-run lead. When the next batter singled, Manager Joe Girardi had seen enough and replaced Severino with Chad Green, who got out of the inning with a pair of strikeouts. Now the question was whether the Yankees could come back.

It didn't take long. After Brett Gardner got on to lead off, Aaron took a two-strike Santana curve ball to center for a single, putting runners on the corners. Two batters later Didi Gregorius belted a game-tying homer to right. In the second, Gardner came up again and slammed a solo homer to give the Bombers a 4–3 lead. The Twins tied it again in the top of the third only to see the Yanks take a 5–4 lead in the bottom of the frame.

Then in the bottom of the fourth Aaron came up once more, this time facing the Twins outstanding rookie right-hander Jose Berrios with one man on base. Berrios was known for having a great breaking ball, a pitch Aaron had some problems with during the year. This time he didn't. The ball hung up there just enough and the big guy hit a screaming line drive to left field that just kept carrying until it landed in the left-field seats for his first homer of the postseason. It gave the Yankees a 7–4 lead and the fans went wild. Aaron was so pumped up that he actually let out a loud yell as he rounded first. It was the most emotion he had shown all year after hitting one out.

With Yankee relievers Robertson, Kahnle, and Chapman shutting down the Twins the rest of the way the Yankees cruised to an 8–4 victory. The win advanced them to the divisional series against the Central Division champion Cleveland Indians. After the game, Aaron was ecstatic, yet he still knew there were important games to come.

"It's a great team win," he said, "but we've got unfinished business. This is what it's about, postseason baseball. The regular season, it's kind of like spring training is over. This is the regular season now. This is what it's all about. This is where those numbers that are hanging in left field (in Yankee Stadium's Monument Park), this is where they made a name for themselves, in the postseason.

"But we can't exhale now because we are going to be facing one of the best teams in baseball. We have to keep this momentum. As for my homer, I was just happy to add two more runs to the board."

Manager Girardi also made an interesting comment about Aaron after the game, and it had nothing to do with his two-run homer.

"There's something about him and the way he carries himself that [makes] you just feel really good when he's around," the manager said. "When he's at the plate, when he's playing defense, when he's standing next to you, waiting for you when you come off the field. You just feel really good when he's around, and I felt that."

The Cleveland Indians had won 102 games during the regular season, including an incredible winning streak of 22 games. They were for real. The season before they went all the way to the World Series where they lost to the Chicago Cubs in the final inning of Game 7. Many felt that 2017 would be the Indians' year. As the two teams got ready for the opening game at Cleveland's Progressive Field, the Indians fine manager, Terry Francona, was talking about—who else?—Aaron Judge.

"From all accounts, he's a really special young man," Francona said. "I didn't get a chance to meet him at the All-Star Game, because I wasn't there, but everybody came back raving about him as a person. We spent a lot of time [talking about] him just because he is so dangerous. I know if you throw it in the wrong place, he's going to hit it a long way.

"But I think as far as the game [of baseball] goes, I think he's really good for the game. When you have young players that are that good and seem to behave and act with a lot of respect like he does, it's really good for the game."

It was almost impossible for anyone around baseball to dislike Aaron. They all saw his friendly demeanor, smiling face, his willingness to sign autographs, and the way he played. It wasn't only his immense talents, but the kind of teammate and team-first guy he was, as well as the positive attitude he always had. To electrify everyone in baseball for half a season, then fall into a deep hole of a slump, only to emerge triumphant on the other end took somebody special. Aaron never changed, never got down on himself, and showed himself to be a leader through it all.

But now it was time for Game 1. Manager Francona decided to hold his ace, Corey Kluber, for the second game and start Trevor Bauer in the opener. It proved a wise decision. The game was almost over before it began. Bauer, with his variety of off-speed and breaking pitches was almost unhittable, while Yankees starter Sonny Gray didn't make it out of the fourth inning. Bauer threw 6.2 innings of shutout ball and his relievers did the rest as Cleveland won easily, 4–0.

It was a game in which Aaron struck out four times, which is sarcastically called the Golden Sombrero in baseball lingo. But as always, he wasn't dismayed.

"Now we've got to just pick ourselves up and get ready for [Friday], Aaron said. "I just missed a couple today. [Bauer] was working the corners well. He was making pitches."

The second game turned into one for the ages, with a controversy that really could have torpedoed the season for the Yankees. The New Yorkers started veteran CC Sabathia against the Indians' ace Kluber. When Sanchez immediately touched Kluber for a two-run homer in the first, it looked as if the Cleveland righty didn't have his best stuff. But CC gave the runs right back in the bottom of the inning. Then when the Indians took a 3–2 lead in the second it was CC who seemed to be in for a short night's work.

Yet in the top of the third, it all came apart for Kluber. Starlin Castro drove in one run and two batters later Aaron Hicks blasted a three-run homer, giving the Yankees a 6–3 lead, finishing Kluber. Two innings later Greg Bird added a two-run shot off Mike Clevenger

and the Yanks had what seemed like an insurmount-
able 8–3 lead, especially with their great bullpen.
At the same time, Sabathia had settled down and
pitched into the sixth inning.

With one out and a runner on first, Manager Girardi
decided to remove his veteran lefty and bring in
young Chad Green, who had been a dominant strikeout machine all year. Green got the second out and
then walked a runner, putting two on with two out.
Cleveland then sent up a lefty-swinging pinch hitter,
Lonnie Chisenhall. Green got two quick strikes on
him, then went inside with a fastball. Chisenhall tried
to check his swing, but the ball seemed to tick off the
knob of his bat right into catcher Sanchez' glove. That
would have been strike three, inning over. But wait.

The plate umpire ruled that the pitch hit Chisenhall
and was waving him to first base. Catcher Sanchez
turned to the dugout and indicated that the ball
had hit the bat, not the player. Managers have 30
seconds to ask for a replay challenge. Everyone
watching, especially after seeing the slow-motion
replay, figured Girardi would challenge. The Yankees
were on the phone with their replay man in the booth
but, for whatever reason, the challenge never came.
It turned out to be a colossal blunder since replays

showed conclusively that the ball did, indeed, hit the bat. The inning should have been over.

Instead, the bases were loaded with shortstop Francisco Lindor coming up. He was one of the Indians' best hitters and it turned out to be the worse-case scenario for the Yankees. Lindor promptly drilled a Green fastball high and deep down the right-field line. The ball hit the foul pole (which is in fair territory) for a grand slam home run. A successful challenge would have left it an 8–3 game, but the non-challenge resulted in the bases-clearing blast that made it 8–7.

It stayed that way until the eighth when Cleveland's Jay Bruce hit a leadoff home run off David Robertson to tie the game at 8–8. After that the Yanks missed several chances to take the lead, including a great defensive play that robbed Aaron of the potential go-ahead RBI in the ninth. From there the game went all the way to the 13th inning with the tension mounting. Dellin Betances was on the mound for his second inning of work after Aroldis Chapman had pitched the 10th and 11th

Outfielder Austin Jackson led off the inning with a single and promptly stole second. Catcher Yan Gomes was up next and slammed a single past third sacker Torreyes down the left-field line to score Jackson with the winning run. The Cleveland crowd went crazy and the Yankees had suffered a backbreaking loss. They were now down, two games to none, and just a game from elimination. The only positive was that the series was headed back to Yankee Stadium for the next two, if necessary.

With another full house at the Stadium the Yanks sent Masahiro Tanaka to the mound to face Cleveland's Carlos Carrasco. Unlike Game 2, this one quickly turned into a pitcher's duel with both hurlers in total control. The game was still scoreless in the top of the sixth when Francisco Lindor came up with a runner on. Once again, he connected on a long drive to right that looked as if it were going to be a two-run homer. But Aaron raced back to the wall, leaped high in the air, stretched his six-foot-seven frame as high as he could and made the catch, taking a home run away from Lindor. The crowd went wild and once again Aaron showed how important he was to the team, even when he wasn't hitting. There was no denying he was all athlete.

The game was decided in the bottom of the seventh inning when Greg Bird slammed a solo home run off the Indians top lefty reliever, Andrew Miller. It turned out to be the only run of the game. Tanaka pitched seven brilliant innings and Chapman got a five-out save to put the Yankees on the board. They now trailed 2–1 with another game set for the Stadium the following day.

Game 4 featured Luis Severino, in his first outing since getting blasted early in the wild-card game, against Trevor Bauer, who stymied the Yankees in the first game of the series. Another full house at the Stadium sat nervously until Severino showed he was back on the beam by quickly retiring the Indians in the first. Bauer, pitching on just three days' rest, got through the first, but found himself in trouble in the second, hurt by some shoddy fielding behind him.

With two out, Starlin Castro reached on a fielding error. Todd Frazier followed with an RBI double to left. Aaron Hicks them drove home Frazier with a single. After a walk to Gardner, Aaron Judge came up. He worked the count full and then whacked a high fastball to left that went for a two-run double. Just like that, the Yankees had a 4–0 lead. And Bauer was out of the game.

Once again Aaron showed his resilience. He had fanned in the first inning and was 0-for-11 in the series with nine strikeouts. It looked like the August slump all over again but he dug in and came up with a ringing double. The second inning set the tone for the game and the Yankees won it, 7–3, with Severino getting the win. Gary Sanchez had a homer and the Indians surprisingly made three errors. Tommy Kahnle relieved an ineffective Dellin Betances and got the six-out save, striking out all three batters in the ninth.

Counting the wild card, the Yankees had now played three win-or-go-home games and had won them all.

"It's been a grind," Aaron said, when asked about the three must-win games. "But we keep winning and that's the most important thing."

Now it was back to Cleveland to decide which team would advance to the American League Championship Series (ALCS), with warhorse CC Sabathia facing ace Corey Kluber. Indians fans fully expected Kluber (who was 18–4 in the regular season and would go on to win the Cy Young Award) to bounce back after his tough outing in Game 2. But it didn't happen.

Didi Gregorius hit a pair of homers in the first and third innings to give the Yankees a 3–0 lead. Sabathia held the Indians scoreless through four until giving up four straight singles and two runs in the fifth. But David Robertson came in to get an inning-ending double-play. Robertson pitched through the seventh and Chapman finished up with a six-out save. The Yanks insurance runs came in the top of the ninth when Gardner delivered a two-out single to drive in one and Todd Frazier scored when the throw to the infield got away. The Yanks won it, 5–2, coming back from the brink of elimination and putting them in the ALCS against the 101-win Houston Astros.

Houston would not be easy. The Astros had a great young core featuring center fielder George Springer, third sacker Alex Bregmann, shortstop Carlos Correa and second baseman Jose Altuve. They had been the best offensive team in the league during the regular season and also had a pair of aces. Lefty Dallas Keuchel had been a Yankee killer for several years, and had shut them out in the wild-card game two years earlier. At the deadline, the team acquired Justin Verlander from the Tigers. He was one of the best pitchers of his generation and at age 34 was still good enough to have a 15–8 record. He was even better with the Astros, going 5–0 with a 1.06 earned run average after coming over. If there was a weakness, it was the 'Stros bullpen. But this series promised to be another tough one.

There was also a kind of sidebar to the series. In Aaron Judge and the Astros' Jose Altuve, the two prime candidates for the Most Valuable Player Award, would be on the same field. While the playoffs don't count toward the MVP prize, many fans wanted to see both star players. Altuve was the American League batting champion with a .346 average, the third time he had won the crown. He also led the league with 204 hits, the fourth time in a row he had done that and surpassed the 200-hit mark. He also had some power with his 24 home runs and 81 RBIs, and he was a threat on the basepaths with 32 steals. Quite a season.

Then here was the size contrast. Altuve was barely five-foot-six, which made him over a foot shorter than the towering Judge. The one thing they had in common was tremendous respect for one another. Altuve had said that Aaron was a great guy and even said he felt the big guy should be the MVP. As for Aaron, he also spoke well of Houston's little sparkplug.

"I've talked to [Altuve] a little bit—what a great guy," he said. "You see what he does on the baseball field, but the type of person he is, you see the passion he has for the game, and it's pretty fun to watch."

There was something else for Aaron to think about, as well. In the five games against Cleveland, he had just a single hit in 20 at-bats and struck out 16 times. Most felt Aaron's bat would have to come alive against

Houston if the Yankees were to have a chance to advance to the World Series. Was this another slump at the worst possible time, or just a couple of bad games? As usual, Aaron was positive and thinking more about the team.

"It's not weighing on me at all," Aaron said, of his batting futility against the Indians. "Every day is a new day. It's just tough in certain situations when you want to go out there and produce for the team and you don't get the job done, especially in a big situation like a Game 5. It's all on the line, win or go home. The past, I can do nothing about what happened in the past or what happened in the regular season, either.

"It's about the Astros and the Yankees, who's gonna go to the World Series. It's just about the team right now. I think the fans are more excited about two great teams getting an opportunity to play."

Game 1 at Minute Maid Park in Houston had Dallas Keuchel opposing Masahiro Tanaka and both starters pitched well. The Astros pushed across two runs in the fourth to take the early lead. In the fifth, the Yanks almost cut it in half. Greg Bird was on second with Aaron at the plate. He worked the count full and then lined a Keuchel offering into left field. Bird, who isn't particularly fast, rounded third and headed home. Left fielder Marwin Gonzalez made a perfect throw to former Yankee Brian McCann who put the tag on Bird. He was out.

After that Keuchel settled down and pitched four-hit ball through seven innings, striking out 10 Yankees. In the ninth, Bird hit a solo homer off closer Ken Giles, but it wasn't enough. Houston had won the game, 2–1, to take a one-game lead in the series. After it was over, the Yankees felt they had missed some opportunities to get to the Houston lefty.

"When you're getting in good counts like we were," Aaron said, "and getting some pitches to hit, you've got to take advantage against a guy like that, because you know you're not going to get many opportunities." Then Aaron again showed his confidence in his team with a lighthearted remark. "We're right where we want to be. We like being in situations where we've got our backs to the wall."

Game 2 proved to be more of the same as Luis Severino matched serves with veteran Justin Verlander early, but it was Verlander going the full nine innings. Houston's Carlos Correa drew first blood for the Astros in the fourth inning, hitting a homer to right that was just over Aaron's outstretched glove, giving his team a 1–0 lead. Severino then was hit on the left wrist by a Yuli Gurriel comebacker in the same inning. Manager Girardi had seen Severino rotating his right arm over his head earlier in the inning and, after the comebacker, removed him from the game. Girardi said later that he was concerned that Severino's shoulder might have been bothering him or tightening up, so he took him out as a precaution.

Todd Frazier tied the game in the fifth with an RBI double, but that's all the Yanks would get off Verlander, who got stronger as the game went on. In the bottom of the ninth, with Aroldis Chapman on the hill and Jose Altuve on first with one out, Correa slammed a double and the speedy Altuve came all the way around to score, helped by Sanchez not being able to handle the relay throw. The walk-off hit gave Houston a 2–1 victory and a 2–0 lead in the series. Once again, the Yankees would be returning to Yankee Stadium in a deep hole.

After the game, many pointed to the Yanks two young stars, Judge and Sanchez, for the team's lack of offense. The two were a combined 0-for-8 in the first two games against Houston and, to take it further, were just 10-for-65 in the playoffs with 34 strikeouts. In addition, the Yankees as a team were hitting just .200 in the postseason. They needed to break out quickly to have a chance of upending the Astros and making it to the World Series.

It was also pointed out that pitchers were throwing Aaron more breaking balls than ever before. MLB.com showed that of 178 pitches to him in the postseason, 96 were breaking balls and that he had swung at 32 of them and missed 25. Manager Girardi said he felt that Aaron's size was also working against him and that he had been getting borderline low strikes called against him.

"I think Aaron falls victim of more strikes called on him that maybe shouldn't be," the manager said. "I think part of that is his height. I've always said I think there's more low pitches called on him. I'm not faulting umpires, but the strike zone changes with body types and he's such a tall guy that maybe it's hard [for the umpires] to adjust a little bit."

Girardi also said that Aaron works hard on hitting the low pitch and feels he'll get better as time passes. With Aaron's history of making adjustments that might not be so far-fetched.

Then came Game 3 at Yankee Stadium and suddenly it seemed like September, because Aaron Judge stepped front and center again, with a little help from his friends. The Yankees would win the game easily, 8–1, behind six scoreless innings from veteran CC Sabathia. So there was no real drama as to the outcome. But other than that, it became the Aaron Judge show, and it wasn't only because of his bat.

In the top of the fourth, Houston's Yuli Gurriel hit a line drive to deep right. Aaron raced to his left, leaped and caught the ball while still in the air, then crashed into the wall, falling backwards and doing a somersault. But he held on to complete a spectacular catch that left some wondering if the wall was all right. Aaron was. That wasn't all. An inning later with a runner on first, the Astros' Cameron Maybin stroked a line drive to short right. This time Aaron raced in, dove in the air and caught the ball while at full extension. His second great catch of the game. In the same inning, he sprinted hard to shallow right near the foul line to snag an Alex Bregman pop-up. Needless to say, the fans went wild.

Offensively, a Todd Frazier three-run homer in the second gave the Yanks the lead. Then in the Yankees fourth with two out and two on, Brett Gardner was hit by a pitch to load the bases. Up came Aaron with a chance to blow the game open. Will Harris then replaced starter Charlie Morton with a vision of a grand slam homer dancing in the fans' heads. Harris spoiled it by throwing a wild pitch to allow a run to score. But then on his fifth pitch of the at-bat, Aaron caught up with him. He hit a screaming liner to left that continued to carry into the seats for a three-run homer and a 7–0 Yankees lead.

After the game, Houston manager A.J. Hinch said this about Aaron: "Judge did what Judge has done 50-plus times, which is hit the ball out of the ballpark when he gets a pitch to hit. Big moment won by Judge. It was his night. He played defense tonight. He did a lot of things well for them, and really was a big difference in the game."

His teammates were also full of praise. "[Aaron] has tremendous belief in himself and confidence," Chase Headley said. "He doesn't let the struggles beat him up."

Todd Frazier summed up Aaron very simply. "He'll go through a wall for you and that's all you can ask for of a teammate."

As for Aaron, he said once again that his approach to each game hadn't changed. "A big change I wanted to make this year was just prepare the right way, prepare the same way and see how it works," he explained. "It worked during the regular season, so why would I change anything in the postseason even though I'm struggling for three or four or five or six games?"

That showed Aaron's patience and confidence that he was doing things the right way, and continuing to do it in the playoffs, and now the Yankees hoped he would go on one of his patented rolls. Game 4 was a big one. A win would allow the Yanks to tie the series, but a loss would put them in a 3–1 hole, and that would be tough to overcome. The opposing pitchers were Sonny Gray for the Yankees and Lance McCullers for Houston. Both had their good stuff and the game was scoreless after five. Then came the sixth and suddenly the Yankee season was again in jeopardy.

When Gray, who had given up just one hit, walked a batter in the sixth he was pulled in favor of David Robertson, who had been outstanding late in the season and into the postseason. But not tonight. He loaded the bases, and, with one out, Yuli Gurriel cleared them with a three-run double. The 3–0 game became 4–0 in the top of the seventh when an error by Starlin Castro led to an unearned run. The Yanks now had nine outs left to mount a rally.

Aaron was the first batter up in the bottom of the seventh. McCullers was still in there, and this time the big guy got him, hitting a moonshot into Monument Park, a drive measured at 427 feet. It knocked McCullers out of the game and gave the Yankees life. Later in the inning Sanchez drove in a second run with a sacrifice fly, cutting the lead to 4–2. Then came the Yanks' eighth.

Frazier started it off with a single, followed by a hit by Headley, who stumbled between first and second, but somehow made it to second with a headfirst slide. Gardner delivered one run with a groundout and then here came Aaron again. This time he tied the game with a booming double off the left field wall. Gregorius followed with another base hit to put runners on the corners and then Sanchez settled matters, driving both runners home with a double in the right center field gap. The Yankees had turned a 4–0 deficit into a 6–4 lead. Aroldis Chapman closed it out in the ninth and the Bombers had tied the series at two games apiece.

Game 5 wouldn't be easy The Astros had Dallas Keuchel on the mound, a guy with a 1.09 career earned run average against the Yankees. The New Yorkers countered with Masahiro Tanaka, who had been pitching very well in the postseason. Tanaka continued his dominance; Keuchel didn't. He would give up four runs on seven hits in just four-and-two-thirds innings.

Greg Bird started the party with a two-out RBI single in the second. Then it was Aaron's turn. He continued his good hitting with an RBI double in the third, while Sanchez and Gregorius added RBI singles in the fifth. Sanchez closed the scoring with a solo homer off reliever Brad Peacock in the seventh. Meanwhile Tanaka threw seven innings of three-hit shutout ball, striking out eight over seven brilliant innings. The Yankees won it, 5–0, to sweep the three games at the Stadium and take a 3–2 lead in the series. Not only were they one game away from going to the World Series, but they also had won all six postseason games played at Yankee Stadium. The problem was they still had to win one at Houston.

Aaron had now hit safely in four of his last five games, driving in six runs in the last three. He had a double and a walk in Game 5, prompting Todd Frazier to describe what happens with the team when Aaron hits. "It calms everyone down. When he's hitting, it helps us at the bottom of the lineup because we're not trying to do too much."

As for Aaron, his attitude simply hadn't changed since day one. "I feel the same as I've felt all year," he said.

"I'm just trying to get productive hits with runners on base. That's the biggest thing. It doesn't matter how you do it." He also detailed just how much fun he was having in the playoffs.

"First postseason and getting a chance to do it in New York, there's nothing like it," he said. "The Stadium is alive. [Our fans] are becoming a force every game. They're in on every pitch. I've never seen anything like it."

Only now it was back to Houston with ace Justin Verlander waiting for them and, as usual, this great clutch pitcher was up to the task. Young Luis Severino matched Verlander for four innings, both pitchers tossing goose eggs. But in the fifth Severino lost command, walking three Astros before Brian McCann drove in one and Jose Altuve two more. That was really all Houston needed as Verlander tossed another seven shutout innings. The Yankees got their only run in the eighth when Aaron blasted a long, 400-foot-plus home run, his fourth of the playoffs, but the Astros finished it against the Yankees bullpen and won the game, 7-1, tying the series at three games apiece.

Now it was time for Game 7. Could the Yanks do what they had done at Cleveland, win the clinching game on the road? So far, that was the only road game they had won during the playoffs. This one was even more important with a trip to the World Series on the line. The pitchers were CC Sabathia for the Yanks and Charlie Morton for Houston. Sabathia was the team's stopper all year, going 10–0 with a 1.69 earned run average in 13 starts following a Yankees loss. They hoped he could do it again. What no one expected was the Yanks continued futility with the bats on the road.

In the second inning of a scoreless game, Houston's Yuli Gurriel hit a shot to deep right. Once again Aaron raced to the wall, leaped high and caught the ball above the wall. He had robbed Gurriel of a homer and hopefully that ignited the Yankees. But it didn't. Sabathia wasn't sharp and lasted just three-and-a-third innings, giving up five hits and walking three. An Evan Gattis homer in the fourth gave Houston a 1–0 lead.

Once again, the Yankees bullpen didn't do the job. The Astros erupted for three more runs in the fifth against Tommy Kahnle, who hadn't allowed a single run the entire postseason. An Altuve homer and a two-run double by ex-Yankee Brian McCann did the damage. That made it 4–0 and this time the Yanks couldn't rally. Morton went five innings and another starter, Lance McCullers finished up. The final was 4–0 as Houston advanced to the World Series.

As for the Yankees, they were going home.

CHAPTER EIGHT

THE AFTERMATH

🏆

EVEN THOUGH FEW PEOPLE CONSIDERED the Yankees contenders at the beginning of the season, the final loss to Houston was a bitter pill to swallow, as much for Aaron in his first season as anyone else on the team. He took it hard:

"It's frustrating. We just weren't able to get the job done. But that's why you play. I wish every game was like that. That's why you grind through 162 [games], for this opportunity. For this moment. There's nothing like it. It's what you dream of. It's why you play the game. We're all going to be thinking about [Game 7] from this

night until opening day. Just keep fighting and getting better in the offseason. Getting as far as we did is really beneficial to us down the road. Just getting a taste of it and getting our feet wet."

While Aaron didn't have a great postseason he did hit four home runs and get a couple of additional clutch hits. He also played great defense, making a number of outstanding catches and robbing opposing players of two home runs. It was the Yankees inability to win on the road that doomed them in the end. They were just 40–41 on the road during the regular season and 1–6 in the postseason. That cost them.

But Aaron was right about one thing. The long run in the playoffs was great experience for the team, especially the young players. Besides Aaron, there was Sanchez, Bird, Hicks, Severino, and Gregorius among others. And with more top prospects down in the minors, the players already there will be able to help them once they make it up to the bigs, or the Show as it's often called.

So the future looks very bright for a team that was supposed to be rebuilding at the beginning of 2017. There would obviously be some changes before the next season, as there always is for the Yankees. A few veterans could leave as free agents; others might not be re-signed to make room for more of the young-sters. And there could be a trade or two. That's always expected in the offseason, but what happened shortly after the season ended wasn't.

The players and Yankees fans heard some shock-ing news. Manager Joe Girardi would not be back in 2018. After ten years at the helm, one World Series win (in 2009), and one win shy of the Series this year, the Yankee brass decided a change was in order. It's sometimes hard to explain why teams change man-agers. Sometimes it's just a matter of getting a fresh voice in the dugout, a new leader, a kind of changing of the guard. There's an old aphorism in baseball that says, managers are hired to be fired. Only a select few managers stay on the job as long as Joe Girardi did. When it happens, the players can't let it affect them. They have to play hard no matter who is running things from the dugout.

Aaron, like the others, admitted he was surprised by the managerial change. "Joe was there for 10 years, had a winning season every year, and he was my first manager," he said. "He was the guy who gave me an opportunity, and he always had my back through the good times and the bad times. It's going to be tough. We're all going to miss Joe, but we'll see who we get for these next couple of years."

When something like that happens it reminds everyone that, while baseball is a game, it's also a business. The players have to roll with the punches. Joe Girardi had called Aaron "a natural leader," and while he'll be in just his second year in 2018, he will be one of the leaders of the team. Aaron also knows he has work to do in the offseason. He'll have to work on pitch recognition, especially identifying breaking balls if he wants to cut down on his strikeouts. He can't expect to hit 50-plus home runs every year, so he's got to find other ways to drive in runs and contribute at the plate. With his work ethic and history of making adjustments, no one is betting against him.

The managerial question was answered in early December when the Yankees named former player Aaron Boone the new manager. Boone played just half a season for the Yankees in 2003 but is remembered for hitting the pennant-winning home run in the ALCS against Boston, sending the Bombers to the World Series. Unfortunately, he tore up his knee playing basketball in the off-season, which led to his release and the Yanks trading for Alex Rodriguez.

Boone, however, has a great baseball pedigree. His grandfather, Ray Boone, was a fine player years back and his father, Bob, was a top catcher and later a manager. Aaron and his brother Bret each had solid playing careers of more than a decade. For the past seven years Aaron Boone had been a baseball analyst for ESPN, but admitted the game was calling him back. Though he had never managed before, he impressed General Manager Brian Cashman and owner Hal Steinbrenner, and won the job over several other candidates. He will give the Yankees a new leader in the dugout.

There was also more business to attend to in the off season. There were the annual awards, and Aaron was soon collecting new hardware. First he was named Sporting News' Rookie of the Year with American League players casting the vote. Aaron got 138 of 140 votes cast, winning in a landslide after his tremendous season. And when the voting for the American League Rookie of the Year was announced, Judge was a unanimous choice of every voter. He was the ninth Yankee to win the prize and the first since Derek Jeter in 1996.

"It's quite an honor," Aaron said. "I'm still sitting back trying to think about what happened this first year. It's been quite a journey—from battling in spring training, to the highs and lows throughout the season, the run we had, coming up short. You dream about playing your first year in the big leagues, and I wouldn't change a thing. It was an incredible year."

That wasn't all. Aaron was one of the recipients of the Silver Slugger Award, given to the best hitter at each position in the league. He was also selected as the New York Player of the Year and would receive the Joe DiMaggio Toast of the Town Award at the New York chapter of the Baseball Writers Association of America's 95th annual dinner in Manhattan on January 28, 2018.

The only award that Aaron didn't win was the American League's Most Valuable Player prize. That one went to the Astro's Jose Altuve, who had a truly incredible season. Aaron did finish in second place, but Altuve won easily. Most felt it was the six-week slump after the All-Star break that could have cost Aaron the award. Fatigue, a shoulder injury, or perhaps a combination of both led to his long slump, something he'll try to avoid in the future. But he was happy for Altuve, who had become a friend, tweeting his congratulations on Twitter.

"M-V-P!!!," he wrote. "Nobody more deserving than you!! Congrats on an unforgettable 2017."

There was yet another honor for Aaron. He was selected to be on the cover of "MLB: The Show 2018," the official MLB video game for PlayStation 4. Major League Baseball made the announcement, another indication that Aaron was considered the new face of baseball. He was the first Yankee to be pictured on the cover since the game was introduced in 2006. The now retired Ken Griffey, Jr., was the featured star on the game until replaced by Aaron.

Then there was the business side of the game. Though Aaron's potential earning power as a star player is almost limitless in the coming years, he was still making the major-league minimum as a rookie. Still a nice amount. But today's athlete's can also make large amounts of money endorsing various products. With the sensational season Aaron had, it was almost inevitable that his agent would be contacted with all kinds of offers. So far, he has inked two deals.

As mentioned, he signed with Fanatics Authentic, a sports e-commerce giant, in August.

That wasn't all, at season's end it was announced that Aaron's first national endorsement deal will be with PepsiCo, the soft-drink company. Aaron is slated to become "the face of Pepsi," obviously a major endorsement deal for him, and it should give him even more national recognition.

"I am very excited to be working with Pepsi," Aaron said. "I always try to find ways to celebrate this great sport with our fans. They're now providing me another way to share my passion for the game."

Then, in late November just before Thanksgiving, there was more news, this one taking fans by surprise and causing some concern. The news broke that Aaron had undergone arthroscopic surgery on his left shoulder in Los Angeles. The surgery was performed by one of the best orthopedic surgeons in the country, Dr. Neal ElAttrache and consisted of removing a "loose body" and cleaning up some damaged cartilage. The feeling is that Aaron will be ready at the start of spring training.

"The shoulder had bothered him throughout the year and when he had an MRI, they found a loose body in there," Yankee GM Brian Cashman said. "Dr. Chris Ahmad [the Yankees team physician] told him that it wasn't something they would move now or recommend doing anything with."

However, Dr. Ahmad suggested Aaron see how it felt over the next few weeks and if he still had discomfort it would be a quick procedure to remove it. The shoulder apparently continued to bother Aaron, and he decided to see Dr. ElAttrache, who agreed with Dr. Ahmad and that's when Aaron decided to have the surgery. So it was obviously of some concern to him, yet Aaron always maintained he was fine during the season. Whether the shoulder was part of the reason for his slump is hard to say. Like former Yankees Captain Derek Jeter, Aaron wasn't one to make excuses. His philosophy was simple: If you can play, you just go out and play. No excuses.

No one was sure when Aaron hurt the shoulder. He made several circus catches during the season, from flipping over a Fenway Park wall on April 26, to slamming into the right-field wall several times during the season. It was obviously bothering him during the slump when he was icing the shoulder after every game. He wasn't icing in September when his resurgence led the Yankees into the playoffs. It wasn't the perfect way to end a marvelous rookie season, but it should help him going into the next season.

Then in mid-December, at baseball's annual Winter Meetings, there was a blockbuster deal that could only help both the Yankees and Aaron. The New Yorkers completed a trade with the Miami Marlins for the National League's Most Valuable player, slugger Giancarlo Stanton, who led the majors with 59 home runs in 2017. The Marlins were in rebuild mode and needed to shed salary. Stanton had a full no-trade clause in his contract and would only go to a few, select teams. The Yanks were one of them, and after negotiations stalled with the Giants and the Cards, New York jumped in and got it done, sending second sacker Starlin Castro and two minor leaguers to Miami.

The thought of Stanton and Judge in the same lineup has already sent shivers up the spines of the Yankees opponents. Add Gary Sanchez, Greg Bird, and Didi Gregorius to the mix and the home runs should be flying off Yankees bats in the 2018 season. Stanton said he looked forward to playing alongside Aaron, adding that he felt the two could only help each other. When discussing hitting in the already potent Yankees line up, the MVP said, "I feel sorry for the baseballs."

As for Aaron, he received a call from GM Cashman before the trade was even completed. The GM wanted to explain the situation and how the two sluggers would be used. It showed the tremendous respect the team had for Aaron, already considering him a team leader. And the big guy's reaction was predictable.

"Hey, I'm pumped," he told Cashman. "This is exciting. If could you pull that off that would be amazing."

It's apparent from the way he has approached everything in his life so far that Aaron Judge is a special kind of person. For a kid from a tiny town in California to wind up in the bright lights of New York City and show the kind of poise, class, humility, talent, and leadership is rather amazing. He thrilled not only the fans of the Yankees with his long home runs and all-around game, but the entire baseball world as well. With his work ethic and burning desire to be the best he can be, fans should expect even more from him in the coming years. For Aaron Judge, the sky's the limit. Perhaps he gave everyone a preview of coming attractions at the season's end when he said:

"We didn't accomplish our goal. We came up short. I think I speak for all of us in the Yankees' organization: We can't wait to get the 2018 season started."

Neither can the fans. And those sitting in The Judge's Chambers will certainly have many more opportunities to hold up their signs and proclaim, "All rise! Here comes Aaron Judge."

ABOUT THE AUTHOR

BILL GUTMAN HAS WRITTEN MORE than 200 books both for children and adults in a long writing career. Included are biographies of many sports stars such as Michael Jordan, Magic Johnson, Ken Griffey, Jr., Brett Favre, and Jeremy Lin. He has also written numerous sports histories, including a book called *Yankees by the Numbers*, and worked with several sports personalities on as-told-to books. Over the years, he has enjoyed interviewing many athletes from all the sports, and more recently was a regular on a sports-talk podcast radio show called *Huddlin' with the Pros*. He is currently also writing a series of novels and novellas about a detective working in 1920s New York City called *The Mike Fargo Mysteries*.